HOW TO CHOOSE A LEADER

HOW
TO
CHOOSE
A
LEADER

———◆◆———

*Machiavelli's Advice
to Citizens*

MAURIZIO VIROLI

PRINCETON UNIVERSITY PRESS
Princeton & Oxford

Published by Princeton University Press
41 William Street, Princeton, New Jersey 08540

In the United Kingdom: Princeton University Press
6 Oxford Street, Woodstock, Oxfordshire OX20 1TR

press.princeton.edu

Jacket art: *Machiavelli in his study.* Stefano Ussi (1822–1901).
Galleria Nazionale d'Arte Moderna.
Alinari/Art Resource, NY
Jacket design by Nicole Caputo

Library of Congress Cataloging-in-Publication Data

Names: Viroli, Maurizio, author.
Title: How to choose a leader : Machiavelli's advice to citizens / Maurizio Viroli.
Description: Princeton, New Jersey : Princeton University Press, 2016. |
Includes bibliographical references.
Identifiers: LCCN 2015043592 | ISBN 9780691170145
(hardback : acid-free paper)
Subjects: LCSH: Political leadership—Philosophy. | Political participation—
Philosophy. | Machiavelli, Niccolò, 1469–1527. | BISAC: POLITICAL
SCIENCE / Political Process / Leadership. | POLITICAL SCIENCE /
Political Process / Elections. | POLITICAL SCIENCE / Civics & Citizenship.
Classification: LCC JC330.3 .V57 2016 | DDC 303.3/4—dc23 LC record
available at http://lccn.loc.gov/2015043592

British Library Cataloging-in-Publication Data is available

This book has been composed in Adobe Jenson Pro

Printed on acid-free paper. ∞

Printed in the United States of America

1 3 5 7 9 10 8 6 4 2

CONTENTS

———◆◆———

◆◆

Why Ask Machiavelli?

With so many competent political commentators at hand it may sound rather extravagant to ask Niccolò Machiavelli for advice on how to choose our representatives and our president. He lived many years ago (1469–1527), had no idea of what a democratic republic would be like, and owes most of his fame to *The Prince*, a book in which he offered his counsel to princes, not citizens.

Americans in general regard Machiavelli as a "teacher of evil," as Professor Leo Strauss put it in his influential book *Thoughts on Machiavelli* (1958),[1] and therefore as a writer who has nothing at all to teach the citizens of a democracy. Before turning their backs to Machiavelli and disregarding his counsels, however, readers should pause for a moment and consider that Machiavelli's political and social ideas had a remarkable impact, directly or indirectly, on the views of America's Founding Fathers. John Adams, for instance, quoted extensively from Machiavelli, and he openly acknowledged an intellectual debt to the Florentine political advisor. Adams even claimed to have been a "student of Machiavelli." In his *Defense of the Constitutions of Government of the United States of America*, he insisted that the "world" was much indebted to Machiavelli for "the revival of reason in matters of government," and praised him for having been the first to have "revived the ancient politics." In his commentary on Machiavelli's *Florentine Histories*, Adams quotes Machiavelli to the effect that, "the most useful erudition for republicans is that which exposes the causes of discord; by which they may learn wisdom and unanimity from the examples of others." Adams criticized Machiavelli for not having adequately understood that a well-framed constitution designed by a constitutional assembly can effectively channel the bad humors of nobles and citizens alike and tame the destructive passions of factions. Yet he boldly asserted that the most revered authorities of republican political thought were all indebted to Machiavelli. Milton, Harrington, and Sidney "were intimately acquainted with the ancients and with Machiavel"; John Locke was a student of the Machiavellian tradition; and Montesquieu "borrowed the best part of his book from Machiavel, without acknowledging the quotation."[2]

Machiavelli has offered American political thinkers and leaders a rich republican theory centered on the principle of liberty as "non-domination," a word that well describes what tyranny is *not*; the conviction that a government of the people is wiser than the government of a prince; the view that the best constitutional arrangement is a mixed government and that a free government needs citizens inspired by a sincere love of country and a strong commitment to uphold the common good; the belief that the Christian religion properly interpreted supports republican freedom; and the persuasion that a fine army composed of citizens is needed to defend the citizens' liberty. In addition, Machiavelli outlined the theory of political revolution that inspired the birth of the Republic of the United States.[3] As Hannah Arendt has rightly noted, Machiavelli is "the spiritual father of revolution in the modern sense," because great modern revolutions originated as "restorations or renewals," in the Machiavellian meaning of "renovations," movements that return the body politic to its origins and thus save it from corruption and death.

The impact of Machiavelli's ideas over the centuries, within very different intellectual and political contexts, can only be explained, I think, by his special understanding of political life. His friends, and even his enemies, recognized this. When he was serving as secretary to the Second Chancery of the Republic of Florence, the governors were amazed by the acumen of his diplomatic reports. His friend Filippo Casavecchia once saluted him as "a greater prophet than the Hebrews or any other nation ever had." After he was fired from his post, Florentine political leaders continued to solicit his opinion in their efforts to understand and predict political events. Francesco Vettori (1474–1539), who served as ambassador of Florence to the papal court in Rome, wrote him, on December 3, 1514: "Examine everything, and I know you have such intelligence that although two years have gone by since you have left the shop, I do not think you have forgotten the art."

The art that Machiavelli mastered was that of interpreting the intentions and the motives of princes and republican leaders. Thanks to this art, he was able to understand real political action, in particular the actions of the founders and redeemers of republics and principalities. He composed all of his works to inspire, educate, and teach great political action: in *The Prince* he sketched the myth of a redeemer of Italy; in the *Discourses on Livy* he offered future generations the political wisdom that had permitted Rome to preserve its liberty and attain an unsurpassed greatness; in *The Art of War* he endeavored to resuscitate the ancient military valor of the Italians. If we elect Machiavelli as our political mentor, therefore, we will benefit from his astute understanding of political life in general and of grand political action in particular, and, made aware of the qualities of a great political leader, we will be in a better position to choose such a leader, if we should encounter him or her.

Machiavelli has yet another virtue of the good political advisor, namely, honesty. After almost fifteen years of public service in which he administered large sums of money, he proudly proclaimed that "my poverty is the evidence of my honesty." None, not even his most ferocious enemies—and he had many of them in his life, as he still does today—have been able to refute this assertion. He also had the habit of speaking frankly even to very powerful people, and he was not afraid of challenging the most revered beliefs of his time. "Contrary to the common opinion, I maintain that . . ." is a phrase that we find many times in his writings. In addition, he rejects the principle of authority, including the authority of Aristotle, still the most respected of all political writers in Machiavelli's day. When Francesco Vettori cited Aristotle's *Politics* to support his ideas on the expansionist ambitions of the Swiss, Machiavelli replied: "I do not know what Aristotle says about confederate republics, but I certainly can say what might reasonably exist, what exists, and what has existed."[4]

Machiavelli based his political judgments (and predictions) on facts (conveniently selected and interpreted) and on reason. They were the product of careful comparisons, historical analogies, evaluations of the consequences of actions, and assessments of the beliefs of political actors and of their motivations for acting in a particular manner. "I do not want to be prompted by any authority but reason," he wrote to Vettori on April 29, 1513. Machiavelli is not only aware, but quite proud of his critical and free style of thinking: "I do not judge to be it a defect to defend any opinion with reasons, without wishing to use either authority or force."[5] In the preface to the first book of the *Discourses*, he asserts that true intellectual advancement calls for the courage to search out "new methods and systems," a courage comparable to that required by explorers of "unknown lands and seas," and it requires as well the will to benefit all. He was also aware, however, that the political truths he had discovered were not definitive, and that others would likely be able to improve on his work: "and although my feeble discernment, my slender experience of current affairs, and imperfect knowledge of ancient events, render these efforts of mine defective and of no great utility, they may at least open the way to some other, who, with better parts and sounder reasoning and judgment, shall carry out my design; whereby, if I gain no credit, at all events I ought to incur no blame."

We also know that he loved his country more than his soul, as he wrote Vettori in one of his last letters. Even if Florence had been ungrateful, unfair, and even cruel to him, he never abandoned it. To the contrary, he dedicated his best intellectual and moral energies to serving the liberty of Florence, and of Italy. In the preface to the second book of his *Discourses on Livy*, he asserted: "It is the duty of every good man to teach others those wholesome lessons which the malice of time or of Fortune has not permitted him to put in practice; to the end that out of many who have the knowledge, some one better loved by Heaven may be found able to carry them out." To teach, at least to teach, what would be of benefit to his country, though he himself had not been able to put it into practice, was the guiding principle of all his works. A powerful reason, it seems to me, to trust his advice.

Machiavelli was ambitious, eager to improve his social status and, above all, to gain glory. But he believed that the right way to attain these goals was to use "public modes," that is, "counseling well and acting well for the common benefit." The way to honors, he stressed, "ought to be opened to every citizen, and rewards proposed for their good counsels and good works, so that they may obtain honors and be satisfied: and when such reputation is obtained through these pure and simple ways, it will never be dangerous." Conversely, he condemned "private ways" of attaining power and fame, namely, by "doing good to this and that private individual by lending them money, marrying their daughters, defending them in front of magistrates, and doing them similar private favors, which make men partisans, and give encouragement to whoever is thus favored to be able to corrupt the public and break the laws."[6]

The fact that Machiavelli lived many years ago assures us that his advice is disinterested. Whether we vote Republican or Democrat, he will continue to repose in peace in Santa Croce in Florence, a most enviable resting place. This fact makes his candidacy as our political counselor even more attractive. If we consider the matter carefully, we will discover that politics has not changed much since his day. Political leaders, and citizens, are guided in their deliberations by the same passions. Some are possessed by the ambition to dominate, some by lust for money, or avarice, or fear, or envy, or hatred; others are led by love of liberty, or compassion, or high-mindedness, or hope. A good student of sixteenth-century politics will be of equal benefit in our own times.

Today, the majority of political advisors believe that abstract models can help us to understand political action; Machiavelli maintains that the true skill of the political advisor is the art of interpreting passions, the passions of individuals and of peoples. To accomplish this difficult task he usually turned for help to history, because for him the political events that occur under our eyes have already happened in the past, in a similar manner. It was thanks to his method that he was able to identify the political problems of Italy and to indicate the right solutions. Italian princes and republican rulers of his time did not, however, listen to him. As a result, Italy fell under foreign domination and experienced three centuries of political and social decline. We can, and must, do better.

On balance, then, it would not be possible to find another counselor as disinterested, competent, and honest as Niccolò Machiavelli, not to mention that he offers his advice freely, out of the pure pleasure of helping us. For to be of assistance to the citizens of the greatest free republic that the world has ever seen would be for him the best of all conceivable rewards, indeed the fulfillment of his life's dream. Can there be any doubt, then, that Machiavelli will work hard to give us the best possible counsel?

I hope readers will not be disappointed to find in these pages mainly cautions intended to help us avoid some of the rather common mistakes we make in our choice of representatives, for they will get a picture of truly excellent political leaders, as well. They will meet statesmen devoted to republican liberty, willing to serve the common good of their country and respectful of the liberty and the dignity of all countries and all peoples; prepared, albeit reluctantly, to set aside moral principles of justice, compassion, and truthfulness, as well as the rule of law, should the safety of the country so require; content to forgo personal success; respectful of the opinions and the concerns of their citizens, but also able to stand above and ahead of them; attentive to the history and the moral and intellectual traditions of their country; and immune from the naive belief that political events can be controlled at will.

Once we are warned against chronic mistakes and we have a clear idea of the most relevant qualities of a good political leader, we can, and must, make up our own minds. No political thinker that I know of, and no scientific methodology, however refined and sophisticated, can relieve us of the burden of choice. "The remainder, you must do it by yourself," as Machiavelli wrote in the last chapter of *The Prince*.

My contribution has been to select from Machiavelli's counsels, to comment upon them, often with the help of citations from his works, and to provide some contemporary examples that confirm their validity. I have been careful to let Machiavelli's voice speak always the louder.

HOW TO CHOOSE A LEADER

I

Citizens ought to "keep their hands on the republic" and "choose the lesser evil."

That is,

Intelligent citizens go to vote, and speak up.

When it is election time, many citizens choose not to discharge their civic duty because they believe that the act of voting is not that important for their lives. Our Counselor's advice on this matter is that citizens must "keep their hands on the republic" and know well "what they should do and whom they can trust."[7] What he means is that wise citizens must be vigilant and keep their eyes fixed on public matters, if they want to prevent their republic from becoming the private possession of a few individuals. Going to vote is one of the means we have of telling our governors and our representatives that we care about the common good. When powerful citizens observe that ordinary citizens do not vote, they persuade themselves that since many of their fellow Americans do not care about the common good, it will be easy to impose their interests and their will, either through cunning or force, or both.

Machiavelli learned how vital it is for a republic that citizens actively participate in political life when he witnessed, between 1512 and 1516, the collapse of the Republic of Florence and the formation of a political regime controlled by the Medici family. When citizens are no longer willing, or capable, of properly executing their civic duties—because they are lazy, or corrupt, or because they believe that smart people are those who do nothing for their republic but nonetheless collect the benefits of others' sense of responsibility—republics decline and die, either because they are invaded or because they fall under the tyranny of one or a few astute and powerful individuals.

Our Counselor also realized that the safest defense of political liberty is the desire of ordinary citizens not to be dominated by the wealthy and the powerful: "They are most fit to have charge of a thing, who least desire to pervert it to their own ends. And, doubtless, if we examine the aims which the nobles and the commons respectively set before them, we shall find in the former a great desire to dominate, in the latter merely a desire not to be dominated over, and hence a greater attachment to freedom, since they have less to gain than the others by destroying it. Wherefore, when the commons are put forward as the defenders of liberty, they may be expected to take better care of it, and, as they have no desire to tamper with it themselves, to be less apt to suffer others to do so."[8]

In addition to voting, we have at our disposal public meetings, rallies, and debates. Machiavelli was the first modern political writer to stress that citizens can and must use these means to express their concerns, particularly when rulers intend to pass laws that transgress fundamental political and social rights. If ordinary people raise their voices to fill the public squares, it becomes much harder for powerful citizens to impose their will and their interests. The outcome of political and social conflicts will then be a reasonable compromise that accommodates, at least in part, the concerns of different social groups. As long as no one can impose one's arbitrary will, the republic remains free. Machiavelli refers, it must be specified, to peaceful social conflicts. He condemns in the strongest possible terms violent social struggles that originate either from the people's wish to dominate the wealthy or from the nobles' desire to oppress the people.

Voting is, however, the most important expression of citizenship—more so in our times than in Machiavelli's day, when the right to choose governors and approve the laws of the republic was a privilege granted to a minority of citizens (to which Machiavelli himself did not belong). Defective as it might be, a democratic republic is preferable to any other political system. An aristocratic republic in which a restricted minority of citizens has the power to pass the laws and choose the rulers almost inevitably degenerates into an oligarchy of citizens who pursue only their self-interest: "because the few always judge in favor of the few."[9] Entrusting sovereign power to a prince is even worse. With all their vices, Machiavelli warns us, the people are better than princes: "[A]s for prudence and stability of purpose, I affirm that a people is more prudent, more stable, and of better judgment than a prince. Nor is it without reason that the voice of the people has been likened to the voice of God; for we see that wide-spread beliefs fulfill themselves, and bring about marvelous results, so as to have the appearance of presaging by some occult quality either weal or woe. Again, as to the justice of their opinions on public affairs, [they] seldom find that after hearing two speakers of equal ability urging them in opposite directions, they do not adopt the sounder view, or are unable to decide on the truth of what they hear."[10] Voting is the most eloquent way of saying that we are loyal to our democratic republic and that we are not interested in its alternatives.

What if no candidate entirely, or at least to a fair extent, convinces us that he or she deserves our vote? In this case Machiavelli invites us to consider that "prudence consists in knowing how to distinguish the character of troubles, and for choice to take the lesser evil."[11] If citizens with high standards stay home, those with lower standards will elect corrupt or incompetent candidates who, once in Congress or in the White House, will foster policies that will damage the common good.

We should therefore vote, and if no candidate is in our judgment sufficiently good, let us vote for the lesser evil. But if we go, what criterion should we adopt to select the best among competing candidates?

———————◆◆———————

"Judge by the hands, not by the eyes."

That is,

Politicians are to be judged by looking at what they are and what they do, not by their appearances.

With this advice, Machiavelli invites us to be wise and to avoid the mistake of believing that politicians are what they pretend to be. This, he adds, is a typical error of citizens with insufficient political wisdom: "the common people are always taken by appearances and by results, and it is the vulgar mass that constitutes the world."[12] If we want to distinguish ourselves from the vulgar mass that is often and easily manipulated, deceived, and misled by corrupt politicians, we must then learn to judge "by the hands."

Easy to say, difficult to put into practice. To "judge by the hands" requires being so close to politicians that we can almost touch them. We need to know well their political biographies and also their personal stories. Very few of us have the opportunity, let alone the desire, to get so close to candidates for Congress or the White House. We see politicians from a distance, if we attend rallies, or on television. They are, moreover, masters in the art of simulation and dissimulation. They can show feelings they do not feel, like grief at tragic events, compassion for the miseries of poor people, indignation at injustices, loyalty to republican institutions, and so on. Or, they can conceal their true passions—thirst for power, egotism, greed, contempt for ordinary citizens. Not to mention their ability to use the power of words to present their actions in the most favorable light or to hide their faults. Pope Alexander V, Machiavelli writes, "never did nor ever thought of anything but to deceive, and always found a reason for doing so. [There was never anyone who] had greater skill in asseverating, or who affirmed his pledges with greater oaths and observed them less, than Pope Alexander; and yet he was always successful in his deceits, because he knew the weakness of men in that particular."[13]

The remedy consists not so much in being close enough to politicians as to be able to grasp who they really are, but rather to look well at *their* hands; that is, to evaluate what they have done and what they are doing. What have they done in their legislatures on the most pressing issues of our republic—on individual rights, political liberty, social justice, immigration, education, and the environment? Have they passed laws that in our judgment help to make our republic more just, prosperous, and decent, or have they opposed them and supported bills that go in the opposite direction? What has been their reaction in the face of political scandals involving their colleagues? It does not take much effort or much time to get this information. And the effort and the time are well spent, if we consider the negative, and even tragic, effects that poor or corrupt political leaders can have on our lives.

Another effective way to assess a politician's quality is to spend a moment examining the people with whom he surrounds himself. Machiavelli offers us this counsel when it comes to the ministers chosen by a prince: "The choice of his ministers is of no slight importance to a prince; they are either good or not, according as the prince himself is sagacious or otherwise; and upon the character of the persons with whom a prince surrounds himself depends the first impression that is formed of his own ability. If his ministers and counselors are competent and faithful, he will be reputed wise, because he had known how to discern their capacity and how to secure their fidelity; but if they prove otherwise, then the opinion formed of the prince will not be favorable, because of his want of judgment in their first selection.[14] If we see that a candidate likes to work with ignorant, arrogant, and pompous collaborators, then we can be sure that he or she is not a person who deserves to be put in office.

What is even worse than being inept at selecting ministers and counselors is being vulnerable to flattery. "I will not leave unnoticed," Machiavelli warns us, "an important subject, and an evil against which princes have much difficulty in defending themselves, if they are not extremely prudent, or have not made good choice of ministers; and this relates to flatterers, who abound in all courts. Men are generally so well pleased with themselves and their own acts, and delude themselves to such a degree, that it is with difficulty they escape from the pest of flatterers."[15] If a politician enjoys adulation, it is certain that he or she will make serious mistakes. Flatterers and adulators always give the kind of advice one likes to hear; they never speak the truth, especially if the truth is unpleasant or calls for difficult or unpopular decisions; they magnify the leader's achievements and belittle the qualities of the opponents. As a result, the political leader is persuaded that no task is too difficult, no achievement is impossible, and this is the surest path to the country's decline. The leader we want must, therefore, be a person who wants counselors who talk straight when they are asked to give their advice.

A good example of Machiavelli's advice put in practice is Franklin Delano Roosevelt's "brain trust." In the spring of 1932, as he was seeking nomination, FDR agreed to the suggestion of putting together a small group of college professors willing to offer some of their time to draft memoranda and discuss policy matters with the president. The "ringmaster of the group, and middleman for their idea," as Arthur Schlesinger described him, was the political economist Raymond Moley of Columbia University. Upon his recommendation, FDR also recruited Rexford G. Tugwell, a specialist on agriculture, and Adolf A. Berle, a prominent expert on corporate finance. As a biographer put it, "Roosevelt did not use the brain trust, or privy council, to provide him with new ideas. He engaged its members to flesh out, articulate, and refine the position he had come to embrace: a readiness to use the power of government to redress the economic ills from which the nation suffered." Wise in choosing his advisors, FDR was even wiser in excluding those who were not up to the task. A distinguished Columbia University faculty member was dismissed because he committed the unpardonable error of submitting the same tariff memorandum to Roosevelt and to his political rival;

another because he was unable to provide "the crisp answer FDR wanted, unencumbered by academic hedging."[16] If some of our candidates show comparable skill in selecting their advisors, we can reasonably assume that they have the temper of the good leader.

III

"It is the common good which makes republics great."

That is,

Wise citizens chose leaders who put the common good above personal and particular interests.

Machiavelli offers us this piece of wisdom in one of his most famous pages. When the common good prevails over particular interests, he writes, all countries and provinces make "most rapid progress. Because, from marriage being less restricted in these countries, and more sought after, we find there a greater population; every man being disposed to beget as many children as he thinks he can rear, when he has no anxiety lest they should be deprived of their patrimony, and knows not only that they are born to freedom and not to slavery, but that they may rise by their merit to be the first men of their country. In these republics, accordingly, we see wealth multiply, both that which comes from agriculture and that which comes from manufactures. For all love to gather riches and to add to their possessions when their enjoyment of them is not likely to be disturbed.

And hence it happens that the citizens of these republics vie with one another in whatever tends to promote public or private well-being; in both of which, consequently, there is a wonderful growth."[17]

If we only consider our self-interest, on the contrary, and we vote for a candidate who promises us that he will lower our taxes, that we can run our companies with no respect for the workers' rights, that we can build our homes with no concern for the harmony of our cities and the environment, we will end up with poor public schools, inefficient hospitals, bad streets and roads, inadequate police, and so on. Moreover, we will have to deal with politicians and public officers who only care about their personal interest and will therefore be corrupt; workers will be at the mercy of their employers; citizens will have no protection against criminality.

As he often does, Machiavelli invites citizens to use their reason to evaluate political and social matters. But many citizens, when they vote, follow their passions rather than reason. According to our Counselor, this behavior is not always blameworthy. If citizens are guided by good passions, like love of country, compassion, and love of justice, they are likely to vote wisely. To explain this important point, Machiavelli turns to the example of the Roman patrician Manlius Capitolinus, put to death by the people of Rome under the charge of sedition: "when he was cited by the tribunes to appear before them and submit his cause for their decision, [the Roman people] assumed the part of judges and not of defenders, and without scruple or hesitation sentenced him to die. Wherefore, I think, that there is no example in the whole Roman history which serves so well as this to demonstrate the virtues of all ranks in that republic. . . . For in all, love of country outweighed every other thought, and all looked less to his past deserts than to the dangers which his present conduct threatened; from which to relieve themselves they put him to death." [18]

If instead citizens are dominated by passions like envy or hatred against particular groups, they are likely to vote for candidates who mean to treat the members of the detested group harshly. For Machiavelli this is a serious mistake, because in cases like this, citizens are keen to forgive their representatives' abuses of power for the pleasure of seeing the people they detest beaten and humiliated. In so doing they give a man, or some men, the power to offend the liberty of all: "When a people is led to commit this error of lending its support to some one man, in order that he may attack those whom it holds in hatred, if he only be prudent he will inevitably become the tyrant of that city.

For he will wait until, with the support of the people, he can deal a fatal blow to the nobles, and will never set himself to oppress the people until the nobles have been rooted out. But when that time comes, the people, although they recognize their servitude, will have none to whom they can turn for help."[19]

Impelled by their hatred and fear (two passions that often go hand in hand) of the socialists, the communists, and the unions, many Italian citizens supported the ascent to power of Benito Mussolini in the 1920s. A similar hatred, extended to the Jews, drove German citizens to back Adolf Hitler in the 1930s. The Italians and the Germans both came to regret their choices. In 1946–1947 strong hate and fear of communists and radicals drove large sectors of American public opinion to support the ruthless and unconstitutional campaign of Republican senator Joseph McCarthy. Later, the U.S. Senate realized that McCarthy's methods had seriously threatened American citizens' liberties and America's international reputation. On December 2, 1954, a Senate Committee censured McCarthy, but the standing of the United States in the eyes of the world had already been seriously damaged and had fueled communist propaganda, which could now proclaim with reason that America was offending against its own principles of individual liberty.

In these cases wrong passions were the cause of serious mistakes. Our reason with its general rules is inapt to guide us to select a particular candidate. But even if we want to vote for persons who are sincerely motivated to serve the common good, how can we be assured that this or that particular candidate is the person we want? It appears that to vote well we need a sort of wisdom that does not consist of general principles and does rely on the ability to access the vast amounts of data commanded only by very skilled political scientists. Let us consider other ways of deciding wisely, in addition to the general principle of judging by the hands and not by the eyes.

IV

***

"Whoever desires constant success must change his conduct with the times."

That is,

The president must be capable of adapting his or her political strategy to changing circumstances, and inclined to do so. Although firmness is generally a virtue, in politics it may be a vice.

Machiavelli clarifies his counsel with these words: "I have often reflected that the causes of the success or failure of men depend upon their manner of suiting their conduct to the times. We see one man proceed in his actions with passion and impetuosity; another with caution and prudence; and as in both the one and the other case men are apt to exceed the proper limits, not being able always to observe the just middle course, they are apt to err in both. But he errs least and will be most favored by Fortune who suits his proceedings to the times, as I have said above, and always follows the impulses of his nature."[20]

As an example, Machiavelli cites the case of the Roman captain Fabius Maximus, who conducted the war against Hannibal with the utmost cautiousness and carefully avoided a direct confrontation. His tactic was the right one, as long as Hannibal was at his full strength. To finish the war, however, took the audacity of Scipio, who attacked the Carthaginians on their own territory.

The history of the United States gives support to Machiavelli's advice with a number of examples that illustrate how a leader's inability to adapt policies to changing contexts damaged the country's reputation and strength and negatively affected American citizens' conditions of life. The first is the off-putting response of the Eisenhower administration to the conciliatory proposal of the Soviet leadership immediately following the death of Stalin on March 6, 1953. As British prime minister Winston Churchill, highly reputed for his political realism and good judgment, put it, "A new breeze [was blowing] on the tormented world" and, he emphasized, "a great hope has arisen in the world." Churchill called for an immediate summit with the Soviets, declaring: "It would be a mistake to assume that nothing could be settled with Soviet Russia unless or until everything is settled."[21]

Even though the negotiations seemed to many to hold promise, Secretary of State Foster Dulles held that the

Soviets had launched a "phony peace campaign," and he labored against their appeasement. As a result, at the end of October 1953 the Eisenhower administration declared that the Soviet leadership had not demonstrated a "readiness to make important concessions" and restated its conviction that an irreconcilable hostility divided the Communist bloc and the non-Communist world. The United States remained determined to continue its efforts designed to achieve "strategic superiority, deterrence, containment, and the calculated, prudent rollback of Communism." American leadership, in Machiavellian terms, did not change its conduct when the political context had changed.

A similar failure to adapt strategies to changing times occurred in the mid-1980s when Mikhail Gorbachev made considerable efforts to create "a more favorable climate" between the two "superpowers." The Reagan administration responded coldly. The president was a resolute anti-communist, and in 1983 he declared that the Soviet Union was the "evil empire" against which the free world, led by the United States, should launch a "crusade." Soviet Union's goal was "the promotion of worldwide revolution and a one-world socialist or communist state." The only morality they recognize, Reagan said, "is what will further their cause, meaning that they reserve unto themselves the right to commit any crime, to lie, to cheat."[22]

Eisenhower's and Reagan's inability to alter their political conduct in view of changing circumstances, as well as their misinterpretation of the new political context, were probably due to their too-rigid adherence to their political convictions. But whatever the case, the two leaders' mistakes had highly negative consequences for the United States. The Cold War could have been ended much earlier, sparing U.S. citizens the tremendous risks of the early 1960s and the hardships caused by the enormous defense budget of the 1980s.

As Machiavelli has written, it is a complicated undertaking for a political leader to modify a strategy that matches his or her beliefs and temperament: "Rome could not therefore have been more favored by Fortune, than to have a commander who by his extreme caution and the slowness of his movements kept the enemy at bay. At the same time, Fabius could not have found circumstances more favorable for his character and genius, to which fact he was indebted for his success and glory. And that this mode of proceeding was the result of his character and nature, and not a matter of choice, was shown on the occasion when Scipio wanted to take the same troops to Africa for the purpose of promptly terminating the war. Fabius most earnestly opposed this, like a man incapable of breaking from his accustomed ways and habits; so that, if he had been master, Hannibal would have remained in Italy, because Fabius failed to perceive that the times were changed."[23]

If political leaders are unlikely to change themselves, then citizens must change their leaders, and they must be wise enough to perceive what sort of president is most in tune with the times. One might suspect that it would be asking too much of ordinary citizens to expect them to have a well-refined sense of their times. But if we asked Machiavelli, he would reply: "[A]s regards prudence and stability, I say that the people are more prudent and stable, and have better judgment than a prince; and it is not without good reason that it is said, 'The voice of the people is *the voice of God;*' for we see popular opinion prognosticate events in such a wonderful manner that it would almost seem as if the people had some occult virtue, which enables them to foresee the good and the evil."[24] This view may seem way too optimistic. History, however, indicates that in the most dramatic times, American citizens were in fact wise enough to select the right kind of persons as their leaders.

V

"How by the delusions of seeming good the people
are often misled to desire their own ruin; and
how they are frequently influenced by
great hopes and brave promises."

That is,

Be very suspicious of candidates who are keen
to attempt bold enterprises.

Our Counselor illustrates this advice with a number of examples taken from ancient history and from his own times. One of his ancient examples is the story recounted by Thucydides in *The History of the Peloponnesian War*: "In the city of Athens in Greece, Nicias, one of the most wise and prudent of men, could not persuade the people that it would not be well for them to make war upon Sicily; and the Athenians resolved upon it, contrary to the advice of their wisest men, and the ruin of Athens was the consequence."[25]

From Thucydides we know that the people of Athens voted in favor of the invasion of Sicily because they accepted Alcibiades's argument that the attack would have inflicted a serious blow to Sparta, their mortal enemy, and because they judged it a courageous and brave enterprise in tune with their pride in Athens's greatness. After a few military victories, the expedition to Sicily turned into a nightmare. The Athenian proponents of the invasion, in particular the ambitious Alcibiades, had simply underestimated the response that the Sicilians, supported by Sparta, would muster, and they had overestimated their own military strength.

American history offers a truly eloquent example of the validity of Machiavelli's advice. In the darkest years of the Cold War, on June 25, 1950, North Korean troops invaded the southern part of the peninsula. Understandably, after Mao's victory in 1949, the Truman administration judged the attack as evidence of the expansionist plans of Communist leadership in Moscow and Beijing; and on September 11, U.S. troops crossed the 38th parallel and moved north.

The rhetoric of the Truman administration was a replica of Alcibiades's arguments in Athens more than two thousand years before. Director of the Office of Northeast Affairs John Allison asserted that the United States had a moral obligation to destroy the North Korean army and fight for Korea's reunification, stressing that the time had come to be "bold" and to "take even more risks than we have already."[26] John Foster Dulles, who later became secretary of state, argued: "Since international communism may not be deterred by moral principles backed by potential might, we must back those principles with military strength-in-being, and do so quickly."

Other prominent political advisors forcefully tried to dissuade the president from launching an attack on North Korea, basing their arguments on healthy political prudence. George Kennan, founder and former chief of the State Department's Policy Planning Staff, stressed that invading North Korea would provoke a Soviet or Chinese intervention. Omar Bradley warned that an attack against North Korea would be "the wrong war, at the wrong place, at the wrong time, and with the wrong enemy." Kennan and Bradley's concurring advice was rejected, just as the old general Nicias's was ignored by the Athenian assembly.

And just like the Athenians in Sicily, American troops accomplished remarkable military victories in the earliest phases of the war. On October 20, General Douglas MacArthur announced the fall of the North Korean capital of Pyongyang and predicted that "the war is very definitely coming to an end shortly" with a complete U.S. victory over the forces of international communism. On November 26, however, a massive attack launched by Chinese "volunteers" forced American troops to retreat. At this point, General MacArthur argued for the deployment of tactical nuclear weapons against Chinese military targets, an action that would have turned the Korean War into a Sino-U.S. war. President Truman dismissed MacArthur as commander of U.S. and U.N. forces.

Bold strategies, appeals to honor, and invocations of high moral principles have great impact in a country like the United States, just as they had in Athens. Yet when these appeals are not sustained by a prudent evaluation of political and military reality, they are a perfect recipe for human and political tragedies. It is much wiser, therefore, to keep Machiavelli's warning always in mind and think twice before voting for candidates who are keen to embark on potentially perilous adventures.

VI

"Men almost always follow the beaten track of others, and proceed in their actions by imitation."

That is,

We should choose as president a candidate who admires the right people and is willing to learn from history.

It is one of the most intelligent ideas of our Counselor that we should recognize the worth of a politician by investigating the models he or she identifies with and is eager to imitate. The more excellent the model, the greater are the chances that our candidate will do a fine job at the helm of the republic. Indeed, if our candidates declare (or indicate by their actions) that their ambition is to imitate a truly outstanding political leader, we should conclude that they entertain the right kind of ambition and, if they are sincere, we should feel reassured of the wisdom of our choice. A politician who fails to equal a great example is better than one who succeeds at imitating a mediocre one. As Machiavelli put it: "A wise man should ever follow the ways of great men and endeavor to imitate only such as have been most eminent; so that even if his merits do not quite equal theirs, yet that they may in some measure reflect their greatness. He should do as the skillful archer, who, seeing that the object he desires to hit is too distant, and knowing the extent to which his bow will carry, aims higher than the destined mark, not for the purpose of sending his arrow to that height, but so that by this elevation it may reach the desired aim."[27]

Though difficult, the imitation of great examples is possible because the passions that orient and guide behavior have not changed much over the centuries. Anger, love, fear, envy, ambition, hope, and avarice still inspire and govern human beings' conduct. If our candidates aspire to follow in the footsteps of great political leaders of the past, they will surely read carefully the memoirs and biographies that narrate the lives and accomplishments of their models: "As regards the exercise of the mind, the prince should read history, and therein study the actions of eminent men, observe how they bore themselves in war, and examine the causes of their victories and defeats, so that he may imitate the former and avoid the latter. But above all should he follow the example of whatever distinguished man he may have chosen for his model; assuming that someone has been specially praised and held up to him as glorious, whose actions and exploits he should ever bear in mind."[28]

A fine example of an American leader who did well by following good historical models is Franklin Delano Roosevelt. From his older (remote) cousin, President Theodore Roosevelt, FDR inherited a sincere love of America's natural treasures and a strong commitment to conservation. "Of all the questions which can come before this nation, short of the actual preservation of its existence in a great war," TR had declared, "there is none which compares in importance with the great central task of leaving this land even a better land for our descendants than it is for us, and training them into a better race to inhabit the land and pass it on." Insisting that only the federal government could "jealously safeguard . . . the scenery, the forests, and the wild creatures," TR doubled the size of the country's national forests and created four national game preserves, five national parks, eighteen national monuments, and fifty-one federal bird sanctuaries.

Inspired by Theodore Roosevelt's example, FDR during his first one hundred days as president issued executive orders transferring sixty-four national monuments to the National Park Service, thus doubling the amount of land the service stewarded. He provided the extra funds required to create the Great Smoky Mountain and Everglades national parks and made sure they would be preserved as wilderness areas. He fought the timber industry over logging in Olympic National Park, blocked utility company plans to convert John Muir's beloved Kings Canyon in California into a hydroelectric plant, and proposed that the Department of the Interior be reorganized and renamed the Department of Conservation.

Another important model for FDR was Woodrow Wilson. Service in Wilson's Navy Department, historian John Milton Cooper writes, transformed FDR into "a thoroughgoing political professional," in the good sense of the word. He watched Wilson expand economic opportunity by lowering tariffs, regulating trusts, and relaxing the gold standard to make credit more available and the nation's currency more flexible. He learned the importance of a strong (but not too independent) cabinet in persuading Congress to adopt administration policy, and he came to understand the critical role a president's vision can play in mobilizing popular support. Interestingly, however, FDR learned more about leadership from Wilson's most notable failure—the Senate's rejection of the peace treaty ending World War I, along with its provision for a League of Nations—than he did from Wilson's legislative successes. Although FDR shared Wilson's belief that a well-structured international governing body could prevent future wars, Wilson's disastrous one-man campaign for the Treaty of Versailles left FDR convinced that vision alone cannot effect change. Before plunging down any path, however worthy, a president has to ensure that Congress and the American public will come along.[29]

Another example of a leader who has accomplished great achievements by following a good model is President Barack Obama. In a July 2011 town hall meeting at the University of Maryland, President Obama stressed that he had learned how to pursue principled compromises, a skill that enabled him to achieve remarkable political results, from Abraham Lincoln: "I think it's fair to say that Abraham Lincoln had convictions. But he constantly was making concessions and compromises. I've got the Emancipation Proclamation hanging up in the Oval Office, and if you read that document—for those of you who have not read it—it doesn't emancipate everybody. It actually declares [that] the slaves who are in areas that have rebelled against the Union are free, but it carves out various provinces, various parts of various states, that are still in the Union, [and it says to them,] you can keep your slaves. Now, think about that. . . . 'The Great Emancipator' was making a compromise in the Emancipation Proclamation because he thought it was necessary in terms of advancing the goals of preserving the Union and winning the war. And then, ultimately, after the war was completed, you then had the 13th and 14th and 15th amendments. So, you know what, if Abraham Lincoln could make some compromises as part of governance, then surely we can make some compromises when it comes to handling our budget."[30]

In addition to great examples, political wisdom derives also from a knowledge of history. History, Machiavelli believed, often repeats itself, in the sense that political leaders and citizens often face problems that have already emerged, in a more or less similar fashion, in the past. This means that with the help of historical analogies we can recognize and understand what is going on before our eyes, and we can learn both from past errors and past successes. "Whoever considers the past and the present will readily observe that all cities and all peoples are and ever have been animated by the same desires and the same passions; so that it is easy, by diligent study of the past, to foresee what is likely to happen in the future in any republic, and to apply those remedies that were used by the ancients, or, not finding any that were employed by them, to devise new ones from the similarity of the events. But as such considerations are neglected or not understood by most of those who read, or, if understood by these, are unknown by those who govern, it follows that the same troubles generally recur in all republics."[31]

This advice of our Counselor must be accompanied here by a few words of caution concerning the use of historical analogies. As another great political writer of the Renaissance, Francesco Guicciardini, put it, it takes sharp and discerning eyes to correctly identify analogies between past and present events. A small difference between two political contexts makes all the difference in the world, and solutions that worked in the past can be totally inadequate, indeed damaging, when applied to the present. Moreover, it is utterly foolish to follow but one political model, as Machiavelli was doing with his beloved Romans.[32] Guicciardini's warnings must be considered carefully. Yet what is most important for our purpose is that we should place our trust in candidates who would faithfully imitate great historical examples and who are keen to learn from history over candidates who follow no models or, worse, follow dubious models and who believe that history is irrelevant for political purposes.

VII

"Great men and powerful republics preserve an equal
dignity and courage in prosperity and adversity."

That is,

We must have at the helm of the republic a person
who is not so inebriated by success as to
become abject in the face of defeat.

Machiavelli maintains that life in general, and political
life in particular, is subject to the whims of Fortune. "Understandably," he writes, many believe that "Fortune is an
omnipotent goddess," because "whoever comes into this
life either late or early feels her power." She "often keeps
the good beneath her feet" and raises the wicked, and if
"ever she promises you anything, never does she keep her
promise."[33] If anyone were wise enough to understand the
times, he or she "would always have good fortune or would
always keep himself from bad fortune; and it would come
to be true that the wise man could control the stars and the
Fates." But "such wise men do not exist: in the first place,
men are shortsighted; in the second place, they are unable

to master their own natures; thus it follows that Fortune is fickle, controlling men and keeping them under her yoke."[34]

Yet Machiavelli did not yield to the common opinion that political events are controlled by Fortune or God alone: "I am myself in some measure inclined to this belief [that the affairs of this world are controlled by God and Fortune]; nevertheless, as our free will is not entirely destroyed, I judge that it may be assumed as true that Fortune to the extent of one half is the arbiter of our actions, but that she permits us to direct the other half, or perhaps a little less, ourselves."[35]

Machiavelli's counsel has a rational basis: "Men can second fortune but not oppose it, they can weave its warp but not break it. They should indeed never give up for, since they do not know its end and it proceeds by oblique and unknown ways, they have always to hope and, since they hope, not to give up in whatever fortune and in whatever travail they may find themselves."[36] The true mark of a great political leader is therefore his or her ability to display the virtue of fortitude—that is, a steady and constant spirit that remains calm in good fortune and does not despair in bad. Why steadiness and fortitude are essential qualities of a true leader, Machiavelli explains to us in a few words: "[I]f his fortune varies, exalting him at one moment and oppressing him at another, he himself never varies, but always preserves a firm courage, which is so closely interwoven with his character that everyone can readily see that the fickleness of fortune has no power over him. The conduct of weak men is very different. Made vain and intoxicated by good fortune, they attribute their success to merits which they do not possess, and this makes them odious and insupportable to all around them. And when they have afterwards to meet a reverse of fortune, they quickly fall into the other extreme, and become abject and vile. Thence it comes that princes of this character think more of flying in adversity than of defending themselves, like men who, having made a bad use of prosperity, are wholly unprepared for any defense against reverses. These virtues and vices are met with in republics as well as in individuals."[37]

The best example of Machiavelli's ideas on fortune and fortitude that I know of comes in the words that Abraham Lincoln penned in a letter to Albert G. Hodges (written on April 4, 1864): "In telling this tale I attempt no compliment to my own sagacity. I claim not to have controlled events, but confess plainly that events have controlled me. Now, at the end of three years struggle the nation's condition is not what either party, or any man devised, or expected. God alone can claim it. Whither it is tending seems plain.

If God now wills the removal of a great wrong, and wills also that we of the North as well as you of the South, shall pay for our complicity in that wrong, impartial history will find therein new cause to attest and revere the justice and goodness of God."[38]

To believe that we cannot master political events, and to believe at the same time that the success or the failure of our political plans ultimately depends on God's will, are reassuring signs of great political wisdom. The first belief encourages a healthy sense of self-restraint. The second urges political leaders to seriously ponder whether their cause is truly just and whether they can honestly expect that a just God will be on their side, as I shall try to further elucidate in the discussion of the next advice our Counselor offers to us.

VIII

<hr>

"And although these men were rare and wonderful, they
were nevertheless but men, and the opportunities which
they had were far less favorable than the present; nor
were their undertakings more just or more easy
than this; neither was God more a
friend of them than of you."

That is,

On balance, it is better to have a leader who believes that
we should put our trust in a God who intervenes in this
world to help the cause of liberty and justice.

Whether Machiavelli himself believed in the Christian
God is hard to tell, though I think he did. That he believed,
or wanted to believe, that an omnipotent and just God helps
the founders of states and their redeemers is beyond dis-
pute. In *The Prince* he writes that Italy "invokes God that he
may send someone who shall redeem her from this cruelty
and barbarous insolence." But God, Machiavelli adds, "does
not want to do everything; for that would deprive us of our
free will, and of that share of glory which belongs to us."[39]

The core of Machiavelli's teaching on this delicate subject is that God will not fight for us, but he will be a reliable and forgiving friend of those who fight for justice on this earth. His purpose, on the one hand, is to dissuade political leaders from indulging themselves in the conviction that they can accomplish anything they want without God's help; on the other, to remove the equally pernicious belief that God will intervene to liberate us from foreign domination, tyranny, and corruption. To attain social and political emancipation, we must be prepared to accept our share of burdens. We must do our part and *at the same time* trust God.

I regard this suggestion as a fine prescription for political leadership. When it has been wisely understood and put into practice, the results have been astonishing. The best example I can cite is that of Abraham Lincoln, the sort of political leader that Machiavelli would have loved to meet, because he greatly admired founders of states and redeemers of peoples, and Lincoln was surely both. His views about God's intervention in human affairs are more nuanced than Machiavelli's. As George Kateb put it, "[I]n Lincoln's mind, the idea of all-powerful providence had to compete with the idea of human free choice, which was all too often blameworthy. It is not clear which idea won in the struggle for Lincoln's acceptance. Perhaps neither one ever definitively did, which would be an anomalously inconclusive conclusion for a true believer in God's omnipotence."[40]

Whatever Lincoln's thoughts on free will and God's providence, it seems to me that at least by the time of his second inaugural address, he had come to believe that God could not be on the side of injustice. "It may seem strange that any men should dare to ask a just God's assistance in wringing their bread from the sweat of other men's faces...." Those who commit themselves to justice can therefore put their trust in God, even if human events, in their atrocity, cruelty, and brutality, seem to have no purpose whatsoever: "Yet if God wills that it [the war] continue, until all the wealth piled by the bonds-man's two hundred and fifty years of unrequited toil shall be sunk, and until every drop of blood drawn with the lash shall be paid by another drawn with the sword, as was said three thousand years ago, so still it must be said 'the judgments of the Lord, are true and righteous altogether.'" It was not God's friendship that Machiavelli recommended to his statesman, but rather the kind of faith in God that helps a political leader to accomplish great deeds.

Machiavelli also believed that republics need religious sentiment—a religious sentiment, more precisely, that gives oaths the necessary strength, implants a sense of shame, instills in the hearts of citizens an awareness of their own dignity, inspires courage, and in sum helps to promote a robust morality. This piece of Machiavellian wisdom was one of the fundamental assumptions of America's Founders, no matter whether they took it from his writings or from other sources. In his *Farewell Address*, George Washington, to cite a well-known example, eloquently restated the view that no sound moral life can be expected in an irreligious people: "Of all the dispositions and habits, which lead to political prosperity, Religion and morality are indispensable supports. In vain would that man claim the tribute of Patriotism, who should labor to subvert these great Pillars of human happiness, these firmest props of the duties of Men and citizens. The mere Politician, equally with the pious man, ought to respect and to cherish them. A volume could not trace all their connections with private and public felicity. Let it simply be asked, where is the security for property, for reputation, for life, if the sense of religious obligation *desert* the oaths, which are the instruments of investigation in Courts of Justice? And let us with caution indulge the supposition, that morality can be maintained without religion. Whatever may be conceded to the influence of refined education on minds of peculiar structure, reason and experience both forbid us to expect, that National morality can prevail in exclusion of religious principle."

There are fine political leaders who do not believe in any revealed religion, and, if asked, would assert that they conduct their lives following only the commands of their conscience. It is also true, however, that citizens and leaders who adhere to a revealed religion that teaches compassion, toleration, and civic responsibility offer thereby a kind of guarantee that they will honorably discharge their duties. What we should fear are political leaders who have neither solid moral principles nor sound religious beliefs. Leaders of that sort dominated Italy in Machiavelli's times (and in later times). As a consequence, he tells us, Italy fell into a miserable social and political condition.

IX

---◆◆---

"For it is the duty of any good man to teach others
that good which the malignity of the times and
of fortune has prevented his doing himself; so
that amongst the many capable ones whom
he has instructed, someone perhaps, more
favored by Heaven, may perform it."

That is,

We must look for a president who cares for his
repute with future generations and has the
ambition to attain true glory.

By the time he had composed his major political works, *The
Prince* and the *Discourses on Livy*, around 1520, Machiavelli
realized that none of his political hopes—the liberation of
Italy from foreign domination, the institution of a well-
ordered republican government in Florence, the rebirth of
virtue—would become reality. Yet he continued until the
last weeks of his life to work, and struggle: "[A]nd I repine
at Nature, who either should have made me such that I
could not see this or should have given me the possibility

for putting it into effect. Since I am an old man, I do not imagine today that I can have opportunity for it. Therefore I have been liberal of it with you who, being young and gifted, can at the right time, if the things I have said please you, aid and advise your princes to their advantage."[41]

The passion that sustained his efforts all his life long was the love of glory—the worthiest of human passions, in his judgment. If they were wise, he writes, men would not allow themselves to be deceived "by a false good and a false glory," but would instead follow the way that "after death renders them glorious" and eschew the way that leads to a "sempiternal infamy."[42] He makes a distinction between fame and glory, and includes goodness as a necessary pre-requisite for true glory: "Pompey and Caesar and almost all the Roman generals after the last Carthaginian war gained fame as brave men but not as good ones, while those who lived before them gained fame as brave and good."[43] He praises the pagan religion because it "did not beatify men if they were not full of worldly glory," as were "cap-tains of armies and princes of republics," and he criticizes the Christian religion because it "has glorified humble and contemplative more than active men."[44]

Another distinction of paramount importance is be-tween glory and power. In a well-known page of *The Prince*, where he discusses the example of Agathocles of Syracuse, Machiavelli remarks that "whoever now reflects upon the conduct and virtue of Agathocles will find in them little or nothing that can be attributed to fortune; for, as I have said, he achieved sovereignty, not by the favor of any one, but through his high rank in the army, which he had won by a thousand efforts and dangers, and he afterwards maintained his sovereignty with great courage, and even temerity. And yet we cannot call it virtue to massacre one's fellow-citizens, to betray one's friends, and to be devoid of good faith, mercy, and religion; such means may enable a man to achieve power, but not glory."[45]

This is the standard we ought to keep in mind when we examine candidates. Is their aim to attain power or to gain glory—that is, do they wish to be remembered as good and valiant leaders by the good persons of future generations or not? It is hard to tell, before the facts, and indeed even after the facts. Yet if we listen carefully, we can detect from their words and their actions their true aspirations. Politicians whose only aim is to acquire power and keep it are exclusively concerned with short-term goals and with electoral consensus; political leaders who entertain thoughts of glory look further forward in time and hope to leave behind favorable signs of their passing in this world. One might suspect that a love of glory would encourage thoughtless ambition to accomplish something grandiose, something not inspired by the principle of liberty. But just as we ought to be wise enough to distinguish a political leader who cares only for power (and money and prestige) from a political leader who is eager to attain glory, we ought also to be wise enough to see the difference between a person who longs for true glory and a person who longs only for vainglory.

X

———— ◆◆ ————

"It is very difficult, indeed almost impossible to maintain
liberty in a republic that has become corrupt
or to establish it there anew."

That is,

Since political corruption is one of the most lethal threats
to liberty, fighting corruption must be one of the
top priorities of any serious leader.

By political corruption our Counselor means the citizens'
inability or unwillingness to put the common good above
their personal and their factional interests: an inability
and unwillingness that translates into a widespread disre-
spect for the laws. In a corrupt city, Machiavelli tells us,
". . . the best laws are of no avail, unless they are administered by a man of such supreme power that he may cause
the laws to be observed until the mass has been restored
to a healthy condition."[46] Corruption is also a perversion
of moral judgment and mores that destroys the very foundations of civil life. In the *Florentine Histories* Machiavelli
puts in the mouth of a fine citizen a long speech against

corruption that fully represents his own ideas on the subject: "The general corruption of the other Italian cities, magnificent Signori, has spread to Florence and infects our city daily more and more. . . . There is neither union nor friendship amongst the citizens, unless it be amongst such as are bound together by some villainous crime, committed either against the state or some private individual. And as all religion and the fear of God is dead in all their hearts, they value an oath or a pledge only so far as it may be useful to themselves. Men employ them, not for the purpose of observing them, but solely as means to enable them more easily to deceive; and just as this deceit succeeds more easily and securely, so much greater is the praise and glory derived from it; and therefore are dangerous men praised as being ingenious, and good men derided for being dupes. And thus, do we see in fact all who can be corrupted, and all who can corrupt others, gather together in the cities of Italy. The young men are idle, and the old men lascivious, and every age and sex give themselves up to unbridled habits; and good laws are no remedy for this, being made useless by evil usages. Thence comes that avarice which we see so common amongst the citizens, and that craving, not for true glory, but for those false honors from which flow hatreds, enmities, dissensions, and factions, which, in turn, produce murders, exiles, and the afflictions of the good and the elevation of the wicked."[47]

One of the causes of political and moral corruption is princely government. Peoples accustomed to living under a prince, Machiavelli writes in the *Discourses* (I.16), do not know how to govern themselves and do not develop the habits of citizenship. Equally damaging to civic spirit is the practice of distributing favors: "[A]ttention must be given to the means employed by citizens for acquiring such influence; and these are twofold, either public or private. The former are when a citizen gains reputation and influence by serving the state well with his counsels or his actions. The way to such honors should be open to every citizen, and suitable rewards should be established, that will be satisfactory and honorable to those who merit them. Reputation and influence gained by such pure and simple means will never prove dangerous to any state. But when they are acquired by private means, then they become most dangerous and pernicious. These private ways consist in benefiting this or the other private individual, by lending them money, marrying their daughters, sustaining them against the authority of the magistrates, and bestowing upon them such other favors as to make partisans of them. This encourages those who are thus favored to corrupt the public and to outrage the laws. A well-regulated republic, therefore, should open the way to public honors to those who seek reputation by means that are conducive to the public good and close it to those whose aim is the advancement of private ends."[48]

Extreme social inequality too produces corruption. "Such corruption and incapacity to maintain free institutions," Machiavelli writes, "results from a great inequality."[49] In another chapter of the *Discourses*, he makes the same point even more eloquently: "Those republics which have thus preserved their political existence uncorrupted, do not permit any of their citizens to be or to live in the manner of gentlemen, but rather maintain amongst them a perfect equality, and are the most decided enemies of the lords and gentlemen that exist in the country." By "gentlemen," he means men "who live idly upon the proceeds of their extensive possessions, without devoting themselves to agriculture or any other useful pursuit to gain a living."[50]

Last but not least, Machiavelli stresses that a major cause of corruption is Christian religion when it is interpreted according to "laziness" and not "according to virtue." As it was practiced in his own time, especially in Italy, Christian religion bore the serious responsibility of having made people weak, and therefore an easy prey for wicked men. He also asserts, however, that if correctly interpreted and lived, Christian religion can be a powerful support of civic life: "And although it would seem that the world has become effeminate and Heaven disarmed, yet this arises unquestionably from the baseness of men, who have interpreted our religion according to indolence rather than virtue. For if we were to reflect that our religion permits us to exalt and defend our country, we should see that according to it we ought also to love and honor our country, and prepare ourselves so as to be capable of defending her."[51]

Machiavelli's denunciation of the devastating effects of corruption has found impressive empirical and theoretical support in contemporary scholarship on social capital and social trust. Robert Putnam, for instance, has shown that the more a society is free from political corruption, the more citizens trust themselves and their representatives. As a result, they are keen to work together for purposes of common interest. In "civic regions," citizens "feel empowered to engage in collective deliberation about public choices." Their collective engagement translates into good public policies. When there is "effective social collaboration," citizens are also more likely to overcome their apathy and mutual distrust in order to resolve problems. This means that citizens who live in sufficiently civic communities are not consumed by feelings of exploitation, powerlessness, and alienation.[52]

Where corruption is pervasive, on the contrary, citizens have little confidence in the law-abidingness of their fellow-citizens. Life is riskier and individuals become weary, worn down, disillusioned. They are likely to insist that the authorities should enforce law and order in their communities with greater rigor, and they are liable to be well disposed to a prince who can impose, through force, the authority of the laws. If we want to continue to live in freedom, we must be exceedingly vigilant about political corruption and choose candidates who by their accomplishments and their statements indicate that they are willing to fight corruption with the utmost determination.

"Poverty never was allowed to stand in the way
of the achievement of any rank or honor and
virtue and merit were sought for under whatever
roof they dwelt; it was this system that made
riches naturally less desirable."

That is,

A just republic must reward and encourage its citizens'
virtue and their readiness to serve the common
good regardless of their social status.

The principle outlined by our Counselor is first of all a
principle of justice that descends from political equality. If
all citizens have the same right to elect their representatives and to be elected, to exclude a number of them from
access to public honors because they are poor is an act of
plain discrimination that will produce justified resentment
in those excluded. It is also an utterly unwise way of selecting the political elite. If all citizens have the opportunity to
distinguish themselves by means of their intelligence, their
devotion to the republic, and their courage, it is almost

certain that the very best will attain the highest positions of responsibility, and they will do a lot of good for the republic. A president of the United States of America therefore must be wholeheartedly committed to the principle that the republic must offer all its citizens the same opportunities to be rewarded according to their merit and virtue.

However, Machiavelli also warns us that in times of peace citizens tend to elect astute and ambitious men who make their careers thanks to connections and favors. He explains this piece of political wisdom in a chapter of the *Discourses on Livy* titled "In times of difficulty men of merit are sought after, but in easy times it is not men of merit, but such as have riches and powerful relations, that are most in favor." The history of the United States offers eloquent examples of the value of this advice. The most widely admired presidents emerged in times of war. By contrast, the failure to recognize true virtue and to choose instead wealthy and powerful citizens has proven seriously damaging. George W. Bush, offspring of a exceedingly wealthy and powerful clan, drove the United States into two wrong wars and failed to prevent a devastating economic crisis.

The best example of the intelligent and effective application of the principle of republican justice is the massive program of education and training for returning servicemen, known as the G.I. Bill of Rights, unanimously voted for by both Houses and signed into law by President Franklin Delano Roosevelt on June 22, 1944. As a commentator has put it, the G.I. Bill has truly "changed the face of America" in the sense of making the country a more just place in which to live. Before the G.I. bill, less than 5 percent of the nation's college-age population attended universities. Under the G.I. Bill more than a million former servicemembers gained access to higher education at government expense in the immediate postwar years. In the peak year of 1947, veterans accounted for 49 percent of total college enrollment. Of the 15 million who had served in the armed forces during World War II, more than half took advantage of the schooling opportunities provided by the G.I. Bill.

America became a much better-educated republic than it had been before World War II. A large number of its youth became not only more savvy, but also more self-confident, more hopeful, and more grateful to their country. Because they were treated justly, they became better citizens, and better human beings. Roosevelt's veterans' legislation, David Kennedy wrote, "aimed not at restricting economy but at empowering individuals. It roared on after 1945 as a kind of afterburner of social change and upward mobility that the war had ignited, propelling an entire generation along an ascending curve of achievement and afflu-ence that their parents could not have dreamed."[53]

One of the reason why people love republican liberty, Machiavelli wrote in the *Discourses on Livy*, is that they know that their sons can hope to radically improve their social standing. With the G.I. Bill this hope became a real-ity. We must demand that every U.S. president be whole-heartedly committed to imitating FDR's achievement.

◆ ◆

XII

"In well-regulated republics the state ought to be
rich and the citizens poor."

That is,

A rich treasury makes possible policies designed to
protect the kind of equality that keeps
the republic healthy.

To be sure, economics was not Machiavelli's area of great-est expertise. "Because Fortune has seen to it that since I do not know how to talk about either the silk or the wool trade, or profits or losses, I have to talk about politics," he confessed to his friend Francesco Vettori on April 9, 1513. The very few references to economic matters we find in his works are all intended to downplay the importance of money in political and military contexts. "It is not gold, but good soldiers," Ma-chiavelli stresses time and again," that insure success in war. Certainly money is a necessity, but a secondary one, which good soldiers will overcome; for it is as impossible that good soldiers should not be able to procure gold, as it is impossible for gold to procure good soldiers."[54]

If a candidate for the presidency of the United States were to make the statement "Keep the citizens poor," he or she would be promptly ridiculed from all quarters. Yet Machiavelli's principle that the republic should be rich and the citizens poor contains a political wisdom that should be taken seriously. To begin with, by "poor" he does not mean "destitute"; he means that citizens should enjoy only a modest level of prosperity, so that they can adequately support their children, and be confident that they will not be dispossessed of the fruits of their labor by rapacious governors or by ambitious men. For this to be possible, a country must live in freedom: "Only those cities and countries that are free can achieve greatness. Population is greater there because marriages are more free and offer more advantages to the citizen; for people will gladly have children when they know that they can support them, and that they will not be deprived of their patrimony, and where they know that their children not only are born free and not slaves, but, if they possess talents and virtue, can arrive at the highest dignities of the state. In free countries we also see wealth increase more rapidly, both that which results from the culture of the soil and that which is produced by industry and art; for everybody gladly multiplies those things, and seeks to acquire those goods the possession of which he can tranquilly enjoy. Thence men vie with each other to increase both private and public wealth, which consequently increase in an extraordinary manner."[55]

If a country is not a republic, its inhabitants can hope to attain some measure of prosperity only if they have the good fortune to be governed by a prince willing to do all he can to support his subjects' economic pursuits: "A prince should also show himself a lover of virtue, and should honor all who excel in any one of the arts, and should encourage his citizens quietly to pursue their vocations, whether of commerce, agriculture, or any other human industry; so that the one may not abstain from embellishing his possessions for fear of their being taken from him, nor the other from opening new sources of commerce for fear of taxes. But the prince should provide rewards for those who are willing to do these things, and for all who strive to enlarge his city or state."[56] If we want to follow Machiavelli's counsel, therefore, we should prefer a candidate who believes that the government should actively intervene to sustain the citizens' economic pursuits over one who believes that it should not.

Machiavelli also teaches us, however, that it is utterly unwise to have governors who are prepared to exhaust the treasury to benefit the citizens. Liberality, he warns us, may be a vice: "If you desire the reputation of being liberal, you must not stop at any degree of sumptuousness; so that a prince will in this way generally consume his entire substance, and may in the end, if he wishes to keep up his reputation for liberality, be obliged to subject his people to extraordinary burdens, and resort to taxation, and employ all sorts of measures that will enable him to procure money. This will soon make him odious with his people and when he becomes poor, he will be contemned by everybody so that having by his prodigality injured many and benefited few, he will be the first to suffer every inconvenience, and be exposed to every danger. And when he becomes conscious of this and attempts to retrench, he will at once expose himself to the imputation of being a miser. A prince then, being unable without injury to himself to practice the virtue of liberality in such manner that it may be generally recognized, should not, when he becomes aware of this and is prudent, mind incurring the charge of parsimoniousness. For after a while, when it is seen that by his prudence and economy he makes his revenues suffice him, and that he is able to provide for his defense in case of war, and engage in enterprises without burdening his people, he will be considered liberal enough by all those from whom he takes nothing, and these are the many; whilst only those to whom he does not give, and which are the few, will look upon him as parsimonious."[57]

An empty treasury is threat to a republic's liberty, and the danger is even greater if the republic is weighed down by debts owed to foreign powers. A healthy treasury and political liberty go hand in hand. German free cities, Machiavelli tells us, have treasuries replete with money and are wisely administered. For this reason their liberty is as safe as it can be: "The power of Germany cannot be doubted by any one, for she has abundant population, wealth, and armies. As to her wealth, there is not a community that has not a considerable amount in the public treasury; it is generally said that Strasburg has several millions of florins so placed. This arises from the fact that they have no expenses for which they draw money from the treasury, except to keep up their munitions, which, when once provided, require very little to keep them up. The order established in these matters is really admirable; for they always keep in their public magazines grain, drink, and fuel enough for one year. They also keep a supply of the raw material for their industries, so that, in case of siege, they can feed the people and supply those who live by the labor of their hands for an entire year without loss. They spend nothing for soldiers, for they keep all their men armed and exercised. For salaries and other matters they spend very little, so that every community has its public treasury well filled."[58]

Politics must govern the economy, not the other way around. More precisely, the political leaders of a republic must have as their primary concern protecting their country's liberty. The same concern must guide the conduct of ordinary citizens as well, prompting them to fulfill their civic duties, in particular the duty to pay their fair share of taxes. Once again Machiavelli points to the German free cities of his own times as examples worthy to be followed: "When these republics have occasion to spend any considerable amount of money for public account, their magistrates or councils, who have authority in these matters, impose upon all the inhabitants a tax of one or two per cent of their possessions. When such a resolution has been passed according to the laws of the country, every citizen presents himself before the collectors of this impost, and, after having taken an oath to pay the just amount, deposits in a strong-box provided for the purpose the sum which according to his conscience he ought to pay, without any one's witnessing what he pays. From this we may judge of the extent of the probity and religion that still exist amongst those people. And we must presume that everyone pays the true amount, for if this were not the case the impost would not yield the amount intended according to the estimates based upon former impositions; the fraud would thus be discovered, and other means would be employed to collect the amount required."[59]

If a republic can count on citizens like these, it is highly unlikely that it will ever lose its liberty. If, on the contrary, they care only about their private wealth, they run a serious risk of being enslaved. Citizens who pay their dues, moreover, make greater demands on their governors and their representatives. They are less likely to be deceived than citizens who are themselves accustomed to deceiving the republic and avoiding their civic duties. This means that we should vote for candidates who want all of us to pay our fair share of taxes, not for candidates who are lenient with those corrupt citizens who prefer to keep their money in their bank accounts and let others pay their share. Machiavelli, in sum, connects economy to citizenship and politics rather than venerating it as the supreme God. Upon careful consideration, our incompetent Counselor on economic affairs is in fact not so incompetent.

XIII

"Prolonged commands brought Rome to servitude."

That is,

It is dangerous to keep the same people in
power for a long time.

According to Machiavelli, prolonged military commands
had two negative effects in Rome: "The first, that fewer
men became experienced in the command of armies, and
therefore distinguished reputation was confined to a few;
and the other, that, by the general remaining a long while
in command of an army, the soldiers became so attached
to him personally that they made themselves his partisans,
and, forgetful of the Senate, recognized no chief or authority but him. It was thus that Sylla and Marius were enabled
to find soldiers willing to follow their lead even against the
republic itself. And it was by this means that Caesar was
enabled to make himself absolute master of his country."[60]

Although his remarks refer to military commands, Machiavelli's advice has broader implications, extending to political life. Politicians who remain in power for a long time

tend to form networks of private allegiances. Through favors and contacts, they often manage to attain the support of many citizens who regard them, not the republic, as the principal object of their loyalty. As Machiavelli reminds us, it is quite difficult for republics to build and preserve the loyalty of their citizens: "A state then, as I have said, that becomes free, makes no friends; for free governments bestow honors and rewards only according to certain honest and fixed rules, outside of which there are neither the one nor the other. And those who obtain these honors and rewards do not consider themselves under obligations to any one, because they believe that they were entitled to them by their merits. Besides the advantages that result to the mass of the people from a free government, such as to be able freely to enjoy one's own without apprehension, to have nothing to fear for the honor of his wife and daughters, or for himself, all these, I say, are not appreciated by any one whilst he enjoys them; for no one will confess himself under obligation to any one merely because he has not been injured by him."[61]

Personal loyalties, on the contrary, are extremely tenacious and almost impossible to dismantle. In the *Florentine Histories*, Machiavelli gives us an eloquent example of how difficult, indeed almost impossible, it is to defeat a power that is based on private loyalties. Citizens who are capable of establishing networks of power through favors, like Cosimo de' Medici, are judged by the multitude as being good and generous persons: "The acts of Cosimo which cause us to suspect him are that he aids everybody with his money, not only private persons, but even the state [and] that he supports the citizens in their reclamations upon the magistrates; and that through the good will of the masses, which he enjoys, he has advanced several of his friends to the highest honors. The reasons, therefore, which we would have to adduce for expelling Cosimo would be that he is benevolent, serviceable to his friends, liberal, and beloved by everybody. Tell me now, what law is there against charity, liberality, and love?"[62]

Against Machiavelli's advice that we should not support political leaders who have been in power for a long time, one might argue that political experience is valuable, particularly in foreign affairs. That argument is well taken, but our Counselor has a reply: "We see from the course of history that the Roman Republic, after the plebeians became entitled to the consulate, admitted all its citizens to this dignity without distinction of age or birth. In truth, age never formed a necessary qualification for public office; merit was the only consideration, whether found in young or old men." Indeed, if we see a candidate who is both young and of great qualities, we should not hesitate to choose him or her: "In electing a young man to an office which demands the prudence of an old man, it is necessary, if the election rests with the people, that he should have made himself worthy of that distinction by some extraordinary action. And when a young man has so much merit as to have distinguished himself by some notable action, it would be a great loss for the state not to be able to avail of his talents and services; and that he should have to wait until old age has robbed him of that vigor of mind and activity of which the state might have the benefit in his earlier age, as Rome had of Valerius Corvinus, of Scipio, of Pompey, and of many others who had the honors of triumph when very young men."[63]

Like all Machiavelli's counsels, this too must not be taken as a rule valid in all circumstances. In the *Discourse on Remodeling the Government of Florence*, for instance, he asserts that the Republic of Florence would need a "Council of the Selected" (Consiglio degli Scelti) composed of citizens at least forty years old, with life tenure. As a general rule, however, it is wiser to choose young leaders over candidates who have been in power for long periods of time.

XIV

"I love my country more than my soul."

That is,

It is a good thing for a political leader to be religious, but he or she must be prepared to put the good of the republic above even God's commands, if necessary (whoever his or her God may be).

In principle, the religious faith, or the absence thereof, of a candidate should be completely irrelevant in the choice of the president. In Europe, to investigate the religious belief of political leaders, or to ask that they reveal them, would be considered totally inappropriate. The prevailing mood in the Old World holds that religious beliefs and practices are private matters, protected from public scrutiny and comment. A political leader could openly profess not to adhere to any revealed religion and yet be respected by the citizens.

In the New World the story is different: Americans consider religion, in particular Christian religion in its various denominations, as the best support of political liberty.

"Religion," Alexis de Tocqueville remarked around 1830, "regards civil liberty as a noble exercise of men's faculties, the world of politics being a sphere intended by the Creator for the free play of intelligence. Religion, being free and powerful within its own sphere and content with the position reserved for it, realizes that its sway is all the better established because it relies only on its own powers and rules men's hearts without external support. Freedom sees religion as the companion of its struggles and triumphs, the cradle of its infancy, and the divine source of its rights. Religion is considered as the guardian of mores, and mores are regarded as the guarantee of the laws and pledge for the maintenance of freedom itself."[64]

In America, religion performs well its task of moral education precisely because it stays away from political power. Tocqueville candidly confessed that he was profoundly struck by his discovery that American priests had no political office and were not even represented in legislative assemblies; they even proclaimed proudly that politics was not their business. On the contrary, when religion seeks the aid of governments it loses its power, which consists in teaching and educating by words and by example. On American soil, religion educates citizens to consider their republic a gift of God, and teaches that liberty is a sacred principle that shapes the civil religion of the republic. In the American democracy, where individuals furiously pursue their interests, religion performs an invaluable function by imparting moderation and education. Because in democratic republics the people is the sovereign, the people must be subject to the superior law of God: "Despotism may be able to do without faith, but freedom cannot. Religion is much more needed in the republic . . . than in the monarchy they attack, and in democratic republics most of all. How could society escape destruction if, when political ties are relaxed, moral ties are not tightened? And what can be done with a people master of itself if it is not subject to God?"[65]

Machiavelli, more than three centuries before, had reached a similar conclusion: "And as the observance of divine institutions is the cause of the greatness of republics, so the disregard of them produces their ruin; for where the fear of God is wanting, there the country will come to ruin, unless it be sustained by the fear of the prince, which may temporarily supply the want of religion." From this persuasion he derived the practical advice that "it is therefore the duty of princes and heads of republics to uphold the foundations of the religion of their countries, for then it is easy to keep their people religious, and consequently good and united. And therefore everything that tends to favor religion (even though it were believed to be false) should be received and availed of to strengthen it; and this should be done the more, the wiser the rulers are, and the better they understand the natural course of things."[66]

We must look for a candidate who is at least respectful of his or her fellow-citizens' religious beliefs, if not deeply and sincerely religious. Better still if he or she professes a religious faith that in history has been supportive of political liberty. If no candidate like that is available, however, we must be sure that we do not elect a president who would run against the religious basis of the American republic. We, however, must also be equally vigilant not to vote for a person who believes that the duty of a president of the United States is to sustain, with the power of the laws, a particular religious creed and a particular moral code associated with it. "To love one's country more than one's soul" means that if a piece of legislation enhances the liberty or the welfare of the citizens but contradicts the dictates of the president's faith, then he or she must put the republic's good above the dictates of religious conscience. We must not choose a president who is keen to make the United States of America a community of faithful.

An excellent instance of a fine understanding of the relationship between religion and politics is John Fitzgerald Kennedy's speech at the Greater Houston Ministerial Association on September 1960, in which he declared, "I believe in an America where the separation of church and state is absolute, where no Catholic prelate would tell the president (should he be Catholic) how to act, and no Protestant minister would tell his parishioners for whom to vote; where no church or church school is granted any public funds or political preference; and where no man is denied public office merely because his religion differs from that of the president who might appoint him or the people who might elect him. I believe in an America that is officially neither Catholic, Protestant, nor Jewish; where no public official either requests or accepts instructions on public policy from the Pope, the National Council of Churches, or any other ecclesiastical source; where no religious body seeks to impose its will directly or indirectly upon the general populace or the public acts of its officials; and where religious liberty is so indivisible that an act against one church is treated as an act against all. . . . Finally, I believe in an America where religious intolerance will someday end; where all men and all churches are treated as equal; where every man has the same right to attend or not attend the church of his choice; where there is no Catholic vote, no anti-Catholic vote, no bloc voting of any kind; and where Catholics, Protestants, and Jews, at both the lay and pastoral level, will refrain from those attitudes of disdain and division which have so often marred their works in the past, and promote instead the American ideal of brotherhood."

The United States of America is the most successful example of a republic that has a strong civic religion, is acceptably tolerant, and has been able to preserve a good separation between church and state. To keep it this way, we must look for presidents who love their country more than their soul. If they also believe that the best way to save their soul is to devote their energies to keeping their country free and just, so much the better.

XV

"For where the very safety of the country depends upon the resolution to be taken, no considerations of justice or injustice, humanity or cruelty, nor of glory or of shame, should be allowed to prevail. But putting all other considerations aside, the only question should be, 'what course will save the life and liberty of the country?'"

That is,

The president must be able, though reluctantly, to leave moral principles aside if the safety of the republic so requires, but must resume impeccable conduct as soon as the emergency is over.

It would be utterly foolish on our part to vote for a candidate unwilling, or unable, to put moral considerations aside, if the safety or the liberty of our republic is truly in danger. I stress *truly* in danger because history offers hundreds of examples of rulers who have perpetrated crimes, violated human rights, and practiced corruption on the pretense that they had to do it to save the country from imminent, inescapable, and mortal dangers or fateful damages to the country's interest.[67] When political leaders use the language of necessity or appeal to situations of emergency, we must be particularly vigilant and ensure that they provide solid evidence for their claim. Even if we are persuaded that the safety and the liberty of our republic is at stake, we should nonetheless insist on a convincing argument that a particular immoral decision is indeed necessary to save our country.

With these strong qualifications in mind, our Counselor's advice stands. It might happen that the safety and the liberty of our country is seriously threatened because of a war, or because of a terrorist attack, or because of internal sedition. When this is the case, we cannot afford to have in the White House a person who puts moral considerations, noble though they may be, above the republic's liberty. Pier Soderini, the chief representative of the Republic of Florence under whom Machiavelli served as secretary from 1498 to 1512, refused to take cruel and unjust measures against the supporters of the Medici who were plotting to overthrow the popular government. As a result, Machiavelli tells us, the popular government collapsed, and the Medici returned in Florence and became the de facto princes of the city: "And although his natural sagacity recognized the necessity of destroying them, and although the quality and ambition of his adversaries afforded him the opportunity, yet [Soderini] had not the courage to do it. For he thought, and several times acknowledged it to his friends, that boldly to strike down his adversaries and all opposition would oblige him to assume extraordinary authority, and even legally to destroy civil equality; and that, even if he should not afterwards use this power tyrannically, this course would so alarm the masses that after his death they would never again consent to the election of another Gonfalonier for life, which he deemed essential for the strengthening and maintaining of the government."[68]

Rigorous respect for the laws on the part of a political leader is praiseworthy and wise conduct, except when the consequence of such respect is the death of the republic. When a political leader must face the tragic choice between saving the liberty and safety of the republic and obeying the laws, Machiavelli warns us, they must remember that their acts and motives will "be judged by the result," and that everyone will praise them, if they have acted against the laws "for the good of [the] country," and not for the advancement of any ambitious purposes of their own. If, on the contrary, leaders do not protect the liberty of their country, because they cannot "enter into evil," they will be harshly blamed both in their own times and by later generations.

An example of the necessary violation of justice is President Lincoln's decision, in April 1861, to suspend the writ of the *habeas corpus* in the territory between Washington D.C. and Philadelphia. Washington was at the time almost undefended, and riots were disrupting communications between the capital and the North. In his message to Congress on July 4, 1861, Lincoln justified his decision with a straight appeal to a situation of emergency: "The whole of the laws which were required to be faithfully executed were being resisted, and failing of execution in nearly one-third of the states. . . . Are all the laws *but one* to go unexecuted, and the government itself to go to pieces, lest that one be violated? Even in such a case, would not the official oath be broken if the government should be overthrown, when it was believed that disregarding the single law would tend to preserve it?"

Five years later the Supreme Court ruled that only Congress, not the president, could suspend *habeas corpus*, and that civilians were not subject to military courts even in times of war. In the spring of 1861, however, Lincoln had solid reasons to reluctantly decide upon such a controversial measure. He was also right, however, when he put civil liberties above alleged considerations of emergency and ordered, in 1863, the reopening of the *Chicago Times*, shut down by order of General Ambrose Burnside because of its pro-Confederate positions. Lincoln's words are the best example I know of the right way to think about emergency measures: "Nothing but the very sternest necessity" can ever justify abridging the liberties of a people. "A government had better go to the very extreme of toleration, than to do aught that could be construed into an interference with, or to jeopardize in any degree, the common rights of its citizens." [69]

What Machiavelli is suggesting is that we choose a leader who is not keen at all to behave immorally but is prepared to enter into evil, if necessary. In addition to war and internal sedition, there are less dramatic circumstances when democratic politics do impose on rulers the hard choice between strict respect for moral and legal norms and accomplishing important political goals. A well-known and pertinent example is Abraham Lincoln's conduct in the political struggle he launched to convince Congress to pass the Thirteenth Amendment of the Constitution that permanently abolished slavery in the United States. On January 6, 1865, the Thirteenth Amendment was reintroduced to the House. To have the required two-thirds majority, Lincoln needed the vote of a few Democrats who had voted against the amendment the previous spring. To secure their votes, Lincoln spoke personally with congressmen he judged amenable to changing their vote. Nonetheless, as the day of the vote approached, he was two votes short. These are the words he addressed to his allies in the Congress, the men to whom he had assigned the task of providing the missing votes: "I am President of the United States, clothed with great power. The abolition of slavery by constitutional provision settles the fate, for all coming time, not only of the millions now in bondage, but of unborn millions to come—a measure of such importance that *those two votes must be procured*. I leave it to you to determine how it shall be done; but remember that I am President of the United States, clothed with immense power, and I expect you to procure those votes." To Lincoln's emissaries it was clear, a biographer has noted, that his power extended to "plum assignments, pardons, campaign contributions, and government jobs for relatives and friends of faithful members." What Lincoln in fact authorized, indeed *ordered*, were measures bordering on, if not falling squarely within the definition of, corruption. On the very morning of the final vote, rumors circulated that Confederate Peace Commissioners were on their way to Washington or had already arrived in the capital. Had the rumors gained weight, the Democrats' leadership would have asked to postpone the vote on grounds that the approval of the amendment would irritate the Confederate Commissioners. To save the amendment, Lincoln had to deny that the Confederate Peace Commissioners were arriving. When asked, he promptly replied, "So far as I know, there are no Peace Commissioners in the City, or likely to be in it."[70] The truth is that Lincoln had been informed that the Commissioners were en route to Fort Monroe. His reply to the Congress was insincere at best, a cunning dodge at worst. But Lincoln's insincerity and cunning made possible the approval of the Thirteenth Amendment. He entered into evil, but gained universal praise. We must be sure that our representatives are capable of imitating Lincoln's example, and not that of Pier Soderini.

XVI

◆◆

"The authority of the dictatorship has always proved beneficial to Rome, and never injurious; it is the authority which men usurp, and not that which is given them by the free suffrages of their fellow-citizens, that is dangerous to civil liberty."

That is,

In situations of emergency it may be necessary to legitimately entrust the president with extraordinary powers, and our candidate must be prepared to accept such powers and wise enough to use them well.

If a republic lacks a constitutional provision that enables the legitimate granting of extraordinary powers to its highest magistrate, Machiavelli claims, an external power may be able conquer it or a tyrant to impose his domination upon free institutions.

As usual, he takes his examples from the history of the Roman Republic: "Whenever created according to public law and not usurped by individual authority, [the Dictatorship] always proved beneficial to Rome; it is the magistracies and powers that are created by illegitimate means which harm a republic, and not those that are appointed in the regular way, as was the case in Rome, where in the long course of time no Dictator ever failed to prove beneficial to the republic. The reason for this is perfectly evident; first, before a citizen can be in a position to usurp extraordinary powers, many things must concur, which in a republic as yet uncorrupted never can happen; for he must be exceedingly rich, and must have many adherents and partisans, which cannot be where the laws are observed; and even if he had them, he would never be supported by the free suffrages of the people, for such men are generally looked upon as dangerous."

Dictatorial powers were not dangerous for the republican order because they were strictly limited in time and scope: "Dictators were appointed only for a limited term, and not in perpetuity, and their power to act was confined to the particular occasion for which they were created. This power consisted in being able to decide alone upon the measures to be adopted for averting the pressing danger, to do whatever he deemed proper without consultation, and to inflict punishment upon any one without appeal. But the Dictator could do nothing to alter the form of the government, such as to diminish the powers of the Senate or the people, or to abrogate existing institutions and create new ones. So that, taking together the short period for which he held the office, and the limited powers which he possessed, and the fact that the Roman people were as yet uncorrupted, it is evident that it was impossible for him to exceed his powers and to harm the republic; which on the contrary, as all experience shows, was always benefited by him".[71]

Extraordinary powers must be not only limited in time and scope, but also, and above all, must be granted in full respect for the Constitution. Not to have in place appropriate constitutional procedures for bestowing extraordinary powers exposes a republic to serious dangers. Even more dangerous would be to allow magistrates to attain extraordinary powers in violation of the rules of the Constitution: "And when a republic lacks some such system, a strict observance of the established laws will expose her to ruin; or, to save her from such danger, the laws will have to be disregarded. Now, in a well-ordered republic it should never be necessary to resort to extra-constitutional measures; for although they may for the time be beneficial, yet the precedent is pernicious, for if the practice is once established of disregarding the laws for good reasons, they will in a little while be disregarded under that pretext for evil purposes. Thus no republic will ever be perfect if she has not by law provided for everything, having a remedy for every emergency, and fixed rules for applying it. And therefore I will say, in conclusion, that those republics which in time of danger cannot resort to a dictatorship, or some similar authority, will generally be ruined when grave occasions occur."[72]

A fine example of a substantial refinement, and perfect application, of Machiavelli's advice is to be found in FDR's first inaugural address, delivered on March 4, 1933: "Our Constitution is so simple and practical that it is possible always to meet extraordinary needs by changes in emphasis and arrangement without loss of essential form. That is why our constitutional system has proved itself the most superbly enduring political mechanism the modern world has produced. It has met every stress of vast expansion of territory, of foreign wars, of bitter internal strife, of world relations." And then he added: "It is to be hoped that the normal balance of executive and legislative authority may be wholly adequate to meet the unprecedented task before us. But it may be that an unprecedented demand and need for undelayed action may call for temporary departure from that normal balance of public procedure. I am prepared under my constitutional duty to recommend the measures that a stricken nation in the midst of a stricken world may require. These measures, or such other measures as the Congress may build out of its experience and wisdom, I shall seek, within my constitutional authority, to bring to speedy adoption. But in the event that the Congress shall fail to take one of these two courses, and in the event that the national emergency is still critical, I shall not evade the clear course of duty that will then confront me. I shall ask the Congress for the one remaining instrument to meet the crisis—broad Executive power to wage a war against the emergency, as great as the power that would be given to me if we were in fact invaded by a foreign foe. For the trust reposed in me I will return the courage and the devotion that befit the time. I can do no less."

Constitutional loyalty and executive or emergency powers can go hand in hand, if we are fortunate enough to have a wise president. Our task is to remind political leaders that we expect them, on such a delicate issue, to imitate the finest examples of the past.

XVII

—◆—

"I say that I have never practiced war as my profession, because my profession is to govern my subjects and to defend them, and, in order to be able to defend them, to love peace and to know how to make war."[73]

That is,

The first priority of a president must be to defend and promote peace. If war, including civil war, is inevitable, the president must be prepared to fight, keeping in mind that military victory cannot be gained at the cost of political liberty.

"The principal foundations that all states have, new ones as well as old or mixed," Machiavelli asserts, "are good laws and good arms. And because there cannot be good laws where there are not good arms, and where there are good arms there must be good laws, I shall leave out the reasoning on laws and shall speak of arms."[74] In *The Art of War*, he reiterates the same point: "Because all the arts that are provided for in a state for the sake of the common good of men, all the statutes made in it so that men will live in fear of the laws and of God, would be vain if for them there were not provided defenses, which when well ordered, preserve them, even though they themselves are not well ordered."[75]

When he speaks of arms, Machiavelli means arms composed of citizens that operate under the laws of the republic, not mercenary or auxiliary arms. Republics that educate citizens to military discipline without ever allowing them to use their military skills for their own benefit are successful in warding off corruption. As long as Rome was incorrupt, Machiavelli writes, "no great citizen ever presumed, by means of such an activity, to retain power in time of peace, so as to break the laws, plunder the provinces, usurp and tyrannize over his native land and in every way gain wealth for himself. Nor did anybody of low estate dream of violating his oath, forming parties with private citizens, ceasing to fear the Senate, or carrying out any tyrannical injury."[76] A well-ordered republic must, then, "decree that this practice of warfare shall be used in times of peace for exercise and in times of war for necessity and for glory." If the exercise of the art of war is firmly under the control of the laws, the republic need in no way fear that armed citizens will become seditious. Its arms-bearing citizens are, quite to the contrary, the soundest foundation for its liberty.[77]

To have good armies a republic must train soldiers who feel loyal to its constitution, have a sense of restraint, and are ashamed to violate the rules of justice in war. As good as they may be, soldiers are almost useless if they do not have excellent commanders. As Machiavelli stresses over and over, the key qualities of fine military leaders are loyalty, courage, the ability to change strategy according to circumstances, and the intelligence to predict the enemy's intentions.

Machiavelli's ideas on the right way to organize the army for the defense of liberty finds a remarkable echo in the writings of Alexander Hamilton. Like Machiavelli, Hamilton thought a great deal about the dangers war poses to free government, and especially to the spirit of liberty in the people. "Safety from external danger," he claimed, "is the most powerful director of national conduct. Even the ardent love of liberty will, after a time, give way to its dictates." The casualties of war are not limited to the battlefield: "The violent destruction of life and property incident to war, the continual effort and alarm attendant on a state of continual danger, will compel nations most attached to liberty, to resort for repose and security, to institutions, which have a tendency to destroy their civil and political rights."[78] Unlike Machiavelli, however, Hamilton did not believe that Rome was an appropriate model for America. "All her maxims and habits were military, her government was constituted for war. Ours is unfit for it, and our situation [as a modern, free, commercial people] still less than our constitution, invites us to emulate the conduct of Rome, or to attempt to display an unprofitable heroism." Any attempt to replicate the effectiveness of ancient citizen armies would require imitating Rome's ferocious imperialism or transforming America into a garrison state, or both. Hamilton's proposal was for a peacetime military establishment of a little over three thousand officers and men. Unlike militiamen, these would be professionals with the time to train to become effective soldiers; unlike mercenaries, they would be citizens, with a stake in their country's liberty.

Though different in important details, Hamilton's ideas were inspired by the same philosophy that Machiavelli outlined: the best guarantee of peace and liberty is a fine army composed of well-trained citizen-soldiers and officers loyal to the Constitution, educated to respect the highest ethical standards wherever they are called to serve.

XVIII

—◆—

"An excellent general is usually an orator because, unless
he knows how to speak to the whole army, he will
have difficulty in doing anything good."

That is,

The president of the United States should be a good
speaker, capable of addressing the citizens on issues
of particular importance for the life of the republic,
and capable of addressing the armed
forces as well, in times of war.

Machiavelli regarded eloquence as one of the most important qualities of political leadership: "To persuade or dissuade a few about a thing is very easy, because, if words are
not enough, you can use authority and force; but the difficulty is to remove from a multitude a belief that is unfavor-
able and contrary either to the common good or to your belief, when you can use only words proper to be heard by all,
since you are trying to persuade them all." Useful in times
of peace, eloquence becomes essential in times of war, when
the armed forces and the whole of public opinion must be

moved to support a common effort. Good eloquence, Machiavelli explains, "lightens fear, sets courage afire, increases determination, uncovers deceptions, promises rewards, shows perils and the way to escape them, reproaches, begs, threatens, fills with hope, praises, berates and does everything through which human passions are extinguished or excited."[79]

To be able to persuade the citizens to endure the costs and the sacrifices that a war, even the most just, imposes, the leaders of the republic must be able to adapt their language to the beliefs and language of the citizens. To this effect, metaphors, similes, and historical examples are especially effective. Machiavelli left us a fine example of eloquence when he composed an oration intended to persuade the sovereign council of the Republic of Florence to pass a law that authorized the collection of funds necessary to defend the city threatened by the armies of Duke Caesar Borgia. To make his point persuasive, he cited history: "Every city, every state ought to consider as enemies all those who can hope to take possession of her territory and against whom she cannot defend herself. Never was princedom or republic wise that was willing to let her territory stand in the power of others or which, so letting it stand, thought she held it securely." To give that same concept more urgency, he resorted to a poignant image: "It is not always possible to put your hand on another's sword, and therefore it is good to have a sword at your side and to gird it on when the enemy is at a distance, because afterward another man is too late and you have no resource."[80] In other words, you should arm yourself, not wait for someone else to defend you.

Well aware that the Florentines were in serious danger of losing their liberty, Machiavelli attempted to overcome their self-serving reluctance to part with the money needed for their defense by instilling in them the fear of death. To that end, he recounted a terrifying historical example with which his fellow-citizens were quite familiar: "Many of you can remember when Constantinople was taken by the Turks [1453]. The Emperor foresaw his ruin. He called upon his citizens, not being able with his organized forces to make proper provision. He showed them their dangers, showed them the preventives, and they ridiculed him. The siege came on. Those citizens who before had no respect for the exhortations of their lord, when they heard within their walls the thunder of artillery and the yells of the army of their enemies, ran weeping to the Emperor with their bosoms full of money; but he drove them away, saying: 'Go to die with this money, since you have not wished to live without it.'" Following the rules of political rhetoric, Machiavelli concluded his oration with an exhortation designed to arouse his fellow-citizens' civic pride: "Such a fall I cannot believe in, when I see that you are free Florentines and that in your own hands rests your liberty. For that liberty I believe you will have such regards as they always have had who are born free and hope to live free."[81]

Machiavelli knew very well that eloquence has the power to mask evil intentions. On balance, however, he worried more about the lack of eloquence in political leaders than about its dangers. He believed that the citizens of a free republic were perfectly capable of deciding what was true, even in an assembly dominated by eloquent men: "As to judging things, if a people hears two [equally gifted] orators who incline to different sides, [very rarely do they fail to] take up the better opinion. . . ."[82]

The history of the United States confirms the validity of Machiavelli's counsel. We have had, to be sure, a fair number of demagogues who have succeeded, for a while, at deceiving American citizens by using colorful and manipulative speech to cover their nefarious intentions. But we have had splendid orators as well, who have been able to move, inspire, and stir the country in the most dramatic moments of its life. The obvious example to cite is

Lincoln's Gettysburg Address. "When Lincoln finished his speech—a eyewitness reported—'the assemblage stood motionless and silent.' The extreme brevity of the address together with its abrupt close 'had so astonished the hearers that they stood transfixed. Had not Lincoln turned and moved toward his chair, the audience would very likely have remained voiceless for several moments more. Finally there came applause.' Lincoln may have initially interpreted the audience's surprise as disapproval. As soon as he finished, he turned to Ward Lamon. 'Lamon, that speech won't *scour*! It is a flat failure, and the people are disappointed.' Edward Everett knew better, and expressed his wonder and respect the following day. 'I should be glad,' he wrote Lincoln, 'if I could flatter myself that I came as near to the central idea of the occasion, in two hours, as you did in two minutes.' Lincoln had translated the story of his country and the meaning of the war into words and ideas accessible to every American."[83]

Another example of the importance of having a president capable of addressing the nation with the right words and the right tone of voice is FDR's speech delivered at the University of Virginia on Monday, June 10, 1940. The occasion was a commencement address. But as the president boarded the train he was informed that Mussolini had launched thirty-two divisions against France, already defeated by Hitler. His words were powerful; his voice dripped with scorn and indignation. As he moved to the central and most touching part of his speech, FDR resorted to the formidable metaphor of the prison to explain the fate that awaited America if Hitler and Mussolini, the champions of the "philosophy of force," were to prevail in Europe: "Some indeed still hold to the now somewhat obvious delusion that we of the United States can safely permit the United States to become a lone island, a lone island in a world dominated by the philosophy of force. Such an island may be the dream of those who still talk and vote as isolationists. Such an island represents to me and to the overwhelming majority of Americans today a helpless nightmare of a people without freedom—the nightmare of a people lodged in prison, handcuffed, hungry, and fed through the bars from day to day by the contemptuous, unpitying masters of other continents. It is natural also that we should ask ourselves how now we can prevent the building of that prison and the placing of ourselves in the midst of it."

To further move American public opinion away from the still predominant isolationist mood, FDR employed yet another powerful image to evoke the utmost possible indignation and contempt for Mussolini: "On this tenth day of

June, nineteen hundred and forty, the hand that held the dagger has struck it into the back of its neighbor." The final exhortation was a call for the swift, determined, resolute engagement of the United States on the side of Britain and defeated France: "On this tenth day of June, nineteen hundred and forty, in this University founded by the first great American teacher of democracy, we send forth our prayers and our hopes to those beyond the seas who are maintaining with magnificent valor their battle for freedom."

As Roosevelt's biographer put it, his "'stab in the back' speech marked the decisive turning point in American policy. Though polls indicated that only 30 percent of the nation believed an Allied victory possible, FDR unequivocally placed himself shoulder to shoulder with Britain and France."[84] Equally important to set the right moral spirit for the long and hard war that the American people were about to endure was FDR's tenth State of the Union speech. A year or so after Pearl Harbor, Roosevelt intended to send a reassuring message to the Allies and openly challenge the apparently invincible armies of Germany and Japan: "As Henry L. Stimson, the secretary of war, put it, it was 'the best speech I ever heard him make.'"[85] Of course FDR drew the figure out of a hat, more or less, but the point of the speech was not telling the truth, but to inspire confidence in the American people and its allies, and concern in the enemies.

As the examples I have cited prove, I think, if America had been without a president capable of addressing the nation and, in particular, the army, Americans might have remained isolationist, or they might have entered into the war too late and without adequate preparation. Clearly, Machiavelli was right in stressing the need for eloquence. More importantly, we too must pay attention to the speech of our candidates. We must make a special effort to detect not only if they are eloquent, but if they have the moral and intellectual depth that gives words the power to inspire, to persuade, and to impel the right course of action. It is not always easy to distinguish a refined orator from a truly great speaker. But if we listen attentively, it is possible. Of two candidates, equally good in other respects, we should choose the one more likely to find the right words in difficult times.

XIX

"A prince becomes esteemed when he shows himself either a true friend or a real enemy."

That is,

Neutrality in international affairs should be the exception, not the rule.

Machiavelli explains his advice that a republic should not pursue a policy of neutrality with the following argument: "If two of your neighboring potentates should come to war amongst themselves, they are either of such character that, when either of them has been defeated, you will have cause to fear the conqueror, or not. In either case, it will always be better for you to declare yourself openly and make fair war; for if you fail to do so, you will be very apt to fall a prey to the victor, to the delight and satisfaction of the defeated party, and you will have no claim for protection or assistance from either the one or the other. For the conqueror will want no doubtful friends, who did not stand by him in time of trial; and the defeated party will not forgive you for having refused, with arms in hand, to take the chance of his fortunes."[86]

Machiavelli further clarifies his argument by stressing that to openly take sides is wiser than remaining neutral, even if the state you have decided to support is defeated: "When a prince declares himself boldly in favor of one party, and that party proves victorious, even though the victor be powerful, and you are at his discretion, yet is he bound to you in love and obligation; and men are never so base as to repay these by such flagrant ingratitude as oppressing you under these circumstances would be. Moreover, victories are never so complete as to dispense the victor from all regard for justice. But when the party whom you have supported loses, then he will ever after receive you as a friend, and, when able, will assist you in turn; and thus you will have become the sharer of a fortune which in time may be retrieved."[87]

Machiavelli's wisdom in repudiating a policy of neutrality received dramatic confirmation at the outset of World War II. As a result of widespread concern over the moral and material costs of the U.S. intervention in World War I, Congress in the 1930s passed a number of measures known as the Neutrality Acts, which forbade any direct or indirect U.S. intervention in foreign wars. As France's defeat came near, in the spring of 1940, Churchill understandably turned to President Roosevelt for help. A cable sent on May 15 eloquently conveys the pressing need as the British prime minister saw it: "The scene has darkened swiftly. The small countries are simply smashed up, like matchwood. We expect to be attacked ourselves in the near future. If necessary, we shall continue the war alone. . . . But I trust you realize, Mr. President, that the voice and force of the United States may count for nothing if they are withheld too long."[88]

After France's surrender on June 22, 1940, England was alone in resisting Hitler's seemingly invincible armies. Its need for active and immediate U.S. military support became even more urgent. Much as he wanted to help Britain and the allies, Roosevelt's hands were tied by the Neutrality Acts. To circumvent them, the president first resorted to the so-called "cash and carry" stratagem that allowed the United States to sell weapons, but under stringent conditions: "No sales on credit; no U.S. funding; no bank loans; no American transport." With U.S. help, Britain avoided the immediate danger of being invaded by Hitler. But the economic costs were devastating, as a letter from Churchill explained: "The danger of Great Britain being destroyed by a swift, overwhelming blow has for the time being very greatly receded. In its place there is a long, gradually maturing danger, less sudden and less spectacular, but equally deadly.... The moment approaches when we shall no longer be able to pay cash for shipping and other supplies. While we will do our utmost, and shrink from no proper sacrifice to make payments across the Exchange, I believe you will agree that it would be wrong in principle and mutually disadvantageous in effect if at the height of this struggle Great Britain were to be divested of all saleable assets, so that after the victory was won with our blood, civilization saved, and the time gained for the United States to be fully armed against all eventualities, we would stand stripped to the bone."[89]

Roosevelt was able to turn the "cash and carry" stratagem into the Lend-Lease program that allowed the United States to become "the arsenal of democracy," as he put it in the memorable speech of December 29, 1940, and effectively to meet Churchill's requests. The risk that, due to the provisions of the Neutrality Acts, U.S. help might arrive too late and prove inadequate had been real, with consequences too horrible to contemplate.

XX

"To insure a long existence to religious sects or republics, it is necessary frequently to bring them back to their original principles."

That is,

Our president must be well aware that the right way to introduce political and social reforms in the United States is to rediscover the principles upon which our republic was founded, without ever entertaining the idea of trying radically new paths.

"There is nothing more true than that all the things of this world have a limit to their existence; but those only run the entire course ordained for them by Heaven that do not allow their body to become disorganized, but keep it unchanged in the manner ordained, or if they change it, so do it that it shall be for their advantage, and not to their injury. And as I speak here of mixed bodies, such as republics or religious sects, I say that those changes are beneficial that bring them back to their original principles. And those are the best-constituted bodies, and have the longest existence, which possess the intrinsic means of frequently renewing themselves, or such as obtain this renovation in consequence of some extrinsic accidents. And it is a truth clearer than light that, without such renovation, these bodies cannot continue to exist; and the means of renewing them is to bring them back to their original principles. For, as all religions, the republics and the monarchies must have within themselves some goodness, by means of which they obtain their first growth and reputation, and as in the process of time this goodness becomes corrupted, it will of necessity destroy the body unless something intervenes to bring it back to its normal condition."[90]

By returning to the founding principles of the republic, Machiavelli means reviving the principles of justice that inspired the actions of the founders, most notably the principle of "honoring their good citizens," and, a point that must be emphasized, the principle of respect for the rules of international law. He also means restoring proper religious worship. In his view there is no question that republics need religion if they are to defend themselves from external enemies and keep their morals sound, for as "the observance of divine institutions is the cause of the greatness of republics, so the disregard of them produces their ruin."[91]

However achieved—as the result of a political or military crisis, or as the effect of a law or of the outstanding virtue of a leader—a return to founding principles rekindles in the citizen devotion to justice and religion. A remarkable refinement of Machiavelli's ideas on the necessity to hark back to the founding principles of the republic is to be found in Abraham Lincoln's speech on the Kansas-Nebraska Act at Peoria, Illinois (October 16, 1854). There Lincoln put forth the idea that slavery was an unashamed corruption of the founding principles of the Declaration of Independence: "Little by little, but steadily as man's march to the grave, we have been giving up the OLD for the NEW faith. Near eighty years ago we began by declaring that all men are created equal; but now from that beginning we run down to the other declaration, that for SOME men to enslave OTHERS is a 'sacred right of self-government.' These principles cannot stand together . . . let no one be deceived. The spirit of seventy-six and the spirit of Nebraska, are utter antagonisms; and the former is being rapidly displaced by the latter."[92]

A few years later, in a speech delivered in Chicago on March 1, 1859, Lincoln forcefully asserted that the corruption of its founding principles inevitably produces the death of the republic: "I do not wish to be misunderstood upon this subject of slavery in this country. I suppose it may long exist, and perhaps the best way for it to come to an end peaceably is for it to exist for a length of time. But I say that the spread and strengthening and perpetuation of it is an entirely different proposition. There we should in every way resist it as a wrong, treating it as a wrong, with the fixed idea that it must and will come to an end. If we do not allow ourselves to be allured from the strict path of our duty by such a device as shifting our ground and throwing ourselves into the rear of a leader who denies our first principle, denies that there an absolute wrong in the institution of slavery, then the future of the Republican cause is safe and victory assured."[93]

A return to the founding principles was for Lincoln the only way to save the Union and the only way to save the republic from degenerating into despotism. "Our republican robe is soiled, and trailed in the dust. Let us repurify it. Let us turn and wash it white, in the spirit, if not the blood, of the Revolution. Let us turn slavery from its claims of 'moral right,' back upon its existing legal rights and its arguments of 'necessity.' Let us return it to the position our fathers gave it; and there let it rest in peace. Let us re-adopt the Declaration of Independence, and with it, the practices, and policy, which harmonize with it. Let north and south—let all Americans—let all lovers of liberty everywhere—join in the great and good work. If we do this, we shall not only have saved the Union; but we shall have so saved it, as to make, and keep it, forever worthy of the saving."[94]

In the Gettysburg Address, Lincoln affirmed not only that Americans must rediscover the principle laid down in the Declaration of Independence that all men are created equal. He also described the return to the founding principles as a rebirth of freedom. To be able to rediscover and appreciate anew its founding principles, America must go through a process of self-examination. This aspect of Lincoln's thought has a clear Machiavellian echo, even if Machiavelli's works were not, in all probability, one of his direct sources. My guess is that Machiavelli and Lincoln drew their ideas on a return to founding principles from the same source, namely the Bible. But whether that is true or not, it is a fact that Machiavelli, like Lincoln, describes the process through which a republic rediscovers itself by rediscovering its founding principles as a process of self-examination that enables a republic to become once again true to itself.

Lincoln, however, seems to depart from Machiavelli's teaching when he reflects on the political conditions that are necessary to achieve a rebirth of freedom. Machiavelli maintains that the rebirth can be attained through the initiative of a man of superior character. In the Gettysburg Address, Lincoln suggests a collective effort: "It is rather of us, the living" to engage in the "unfinished work" of refounding freedom. Yet Machiavelli's and Lincoln's intellectual and political perspectives are less distant than they might at first appear.

Machiavelli does not envisage a political leader who does all the work by himself, followed by passive citizens or subjects who obey his orders. He invokes a leader capable of persuading, inspiring, and motivating fellow patriots to commit themselves to the arduous task of political redemption. Lincoln spoke of "us, the living," but he was well aware that the task of leading the country through the arduous process of rediscovering its true principles was upon his shoulders. His example suggests that Machiavelli's *idea* that the right way to infuse new life into the body of the republic is to bring it back to its founding principles of justice and religion is an integral part of American political tradition. When Machiavelli's wisdom has been intelligently interpreted and put into practice, its benefits for the American republic, and for other republics, have been conspicuous.

NOTES

1. Leo Strauss, *Thoughts on Machiavelli* (Glencoe, Ill.: Free Press, 1958).

2. C. Bradley Thompson, "John Adams's Machiavellian Moment," *Review of Politics* 57 (1995), pp. 389–417. See also Karl Walling, "Was Alexander Hamilton a Machiavellian Statesman?" *Review of Politics* 57 (1995), pp. 419–447; and Brian Danoff, "Lincoln, Machiavelli, and American Political Thought," *Presidential Studies Quarterly* 30 (2000), pp. 290–310.

3. On the intellectual features of the American Revolution, see Gordon S. Wood, *The Creation of the American Republic, 1776–1787* (Chapel Hill: University of North Carolina Press, 1969); Bailyn Bernard, *The Ideological Origins of the American Revolution* (Cambridge, Mass.: Belknap Press of Harvard University Press, 1967).

4. Niccolò Machiavelli to Francesco Vettori, August 26, 1513, in *Machiavelli and His Friends: Their Personal Correspondence*, trans. and ed. James B. Atkinson and David Sices (DeKalb, Ill.: Northern Illinois University Press, 1996), p. 258.

5. *Discourses on Livy* I.58.

6. *Discourses on Livy* III.28.

7. *A Discourse on Remodeling the Government of Florence*, in *Machiavelli: The Chief Works and Others*, trans. Allan Gilbert (Durham, N.C. and London: Duke University Press, 1989), vol. I, p. 115; *The Prince* XXI.

8. *Discourses on Livy* I.5.

9. *Discourses on Livy* I.7.

10. *Discourses on Livy* I.58.

11. *The Prince* XXI.

12. *The Prince* XVIII.

13. *The Prince* XVIII.

14. *The Prince* XXII.

15. *The Prince* XXIII.

16. Jean Edward Smith, *FDR* (New York: Random House, 2007), pp. 262–263.

17. *Discourses on Livy* II.2.

18. *Discourses on Livy* III.8.

19. *Discourses on Livy* I.40.

20. *Discourses on Livy* III.9.

21. Stephen G. Walker and Akan Malici, *U.S. Presidents and Foreign Policy Mistakes* (Stanford: Stanford University Press, 2011), pp. 120–121.

22. Walker and Malici, *U.S. Presidents*, p. 7.

23. *Discourses on Livy* III.9.

24. *Discourses on Livy* I.58.

25. *Discourses on Livy* I.53.

26. Walker and Malici, *U.S. Presidents*, pp. 145–146.

27. *The Prince* VI.

28. *Discourses on Livy* I.14.

29. "FDR's Models, Theodore Roosevelt and Woodrow Wilson," chapter I.1 in fdr4Freedoms, accessed November 29, 2015, http://fdr4freedoms.org/wp-content/themes/fdf4fdr/DownloadablePDFs/I_FDRBeforethePresidency/01_FranklinDRooseveltsModels.pdf

30. Frank James, "Obama Cites Lincoln as Principled Politician Who Compromised," NPR "it's all politics," July 22, 2011, accessed November 29, 2015, http://www.npr.org/sections/itsallpolitics/2011/07/22/138619171/obama-cites-lincoln-as-model-of-principled-politician-who-compromised.

31. *Discourses on Livy* I.39.

32. Francesco Guicciardini, *Maxims and Reflections of a Renaissance Statesman (Ricordi)*, trans. Mario Domandi; introduction by Nicolai Rubinstein (Gloucester, Mass.: P. Smith, 1970).

33. *Tercets on Fortune* 25–30.

34. Machiavelli to Giovan Battista Soderini, September 13–21, 1506, in *Machiavelli and His Friends*, p. 135.

35. *The Prince* XXV.

36. *Discourses on Livy* II.27.

37. *Discourses on Livy* III.31.

38. Abraham Lincoln, *Speeches and Writings, 1859–1865* (New York: Library of America, 1989), p. 586.

39. *The Prince* XXVI.

40. George Kateb, *Lincoln's Political Thought* (Cambridge, Mass.: Harvard University Press, 2015), pp. 188–189.

41. *The Art of War* VII.

42. *Discourses on Livy* I.10.

43. *The Art of War* I.

44. *Discourses on Livy* II.2.

45. *The Prince* VIII.

46. *Discourses on Livy* I.17.

47. *The History of Florence* III.5.

48. *Discourses on Livy* III.28.

49. *Discourses on Livy* I.17.

50. *Discourses on Livy* I.55.

51. *Discourses on Livy* II.2.

52. Robert Putnam, *Making Democracy Work: Civic Traditions in Modern Italy* (Princeton, N.J.: Princeton University Press, 1993); *Bowling Alone: The Collapse and Revival of American Community* (New York: Simon & Schuster, 2000).

53. Smith, *FDR*, pp. 584–585.

54. *Discourses on Livy* II.10.

55. *Discourses on Livy* II.2.

56. *The Prince* XXI.

57. *The Prince* XVI.

58. "Second Report on the Affairs of Germany," in *Historical, Political, and Diplomatic Works*, vol. IV, ed. Christian E. Detmold (Boston and New York: Houghton, Mifflin and Company, 1891), pp. 397–398.

59. *Discourses on Livy* I.55.

60. *Discourses on Livy* III.24.

61. *Discourses on Livy* I.16.

62. *The History of Florence* IV.27.

63. *Discourses on Livy* I.60.

64. Alexis de Tocqueville, *Democracy in America*, trans. George Lawrence, ed. J. P. Mayer (New York: Harper & Row, 2000), p. 47.

65. Tocqueville, p. 294.

66. *Discourses on Livy* I.11.

67. For an excellent documentation of massive violations of human rights under the pretense that they were necessary to face a situation of emergency, see Jane Mayer, *The Dark Side: How the War on Terror Turned into a War on American Ideals* (New York: Doubleday, 2008).

68. *Discourses on Livy* III.3.

69. Doris Kearns Goodwin, *Team of Rivals: The Political Genius of Abraham Lincoln* (New York: Simon & Schuster, 2012), p. 523.

70. Goodwin, *Team of Rivals*, pp. 686–689.

71. *Discourses on Livy* I.34.

72. *Discourses on Livy* I.34.

73. Machiavelli puts these words in the mouth of Fabrizio Colonna in his dialogue *The Art of War*. They also reflect, however, Machiavelli's own views.

74. *The Prince* XII.

75. *The Art of War*, Preface.

76. *The Art of War* I.

77. *The Art of War* I.

78. Walling, "Was Alexander Hamilton a Machiavellian Statesman?" p. 438–440.

79. *The Art of War* IV.

80. *Words to Be Spoken on the Law for Appropriating Money*, in *Machiavelli: The Chief Works and Others*, ed., A. Gilbert (Durham, N.C. and London: Duke University Press, 1989), vol. III, pp. 1440–1441.

81. *Words to Be Spoken*, pp. 1442–1443.

82. *Discourses on Livy* I.58.

83. Goodwin, *Team of Rivals*, pp. 583–587.

84. Smith, *FDR*, p. 449.

85. Smith, *FDR*, p. 548.

86. *The Prince* XXI.

87. *The Prince* XXI.

88. Smith, *FDR*, p. 446.

89. Smith, *FDR*, p. 484.

90. *Discourses on Livy* III.1.

91. *Discourses on Livy* I.11.

92. Lincoln, *Speeches and Writings 1832–1858*, p. 339.

93. Lincoln, *Speeches and Writings 1859–1865*, p. 17.

94. Lincoln, *Speeches and Writings 1832–1858*, pp. 339–340.

SOURCES OF THE QUOTATIONS

NOTE ON THE TEXTS

For Machiavelli's works I have used Niccolò Machiavelli, *Opere*, a cura di Corrado Vivanti. 4 vols. Turin: Einaudi, 1999–2005.

I have used as well the following English translations:

Machiavelli and His Friends: Their Personal Correspondence, translated and edited by James B. Atkinson and David Sices. DeKalb, Ill.: Northern Illinois University Press, 1996.

The Historical, Political, and Diplomatic Writings of Niccolò Machiavelli, translated and edited by Christian E. Detmold. Vols. I and III, Boston: James R. Osgood Company, 1882; vols. II and IV, Boston and New York: Houghton, Mifflin and Company, 1891.

Machiavelli: The Chief Works and Others, translated and edited by Allan Gilbert. Vol. I: *A Discourse on Remodeling the Government of Florence*; vol. II: *The Art of War; Tercets on Ambition; Tercets on Ingratitude or Envy; Tercets on Fortune*; vol. III: *Words to Be Spoken on the Law for Appropriating Money*, Durham, NC and London: Duke University Press, 1989.